MAKING INEXPENSIVE LIQUEURS

MAKING INEXPENSIVE LIQUEURS

REN BELLIS

AMATEUR WINEMAKER

Published by

Amateur Winemaker

Argus Books Limited
1 Golden Square
London W1R 3AB
England

1st Impression 1975
2nd Impression 1978
3rd Impression 1979
4th Impression 1981
5th Impression 1984
Reprinted 1986

ISBN 0 900841 43 5

Printed in Great Britain by
The Garden City Press Ltd.,
Pixmore Avenue, Letchworth, Herts

CONTENTS

Foreword

THE word "liqueur", merely the French equivalent of our own word "liquor", has a rich and expansive sound to it, conjuring up a mind-picture of extravagant living.

The commercial product is, indeed, so priced as to be beyond the scope of the average household budget except, perhaps, for the occasional high-days and holidays when expense becomes a secondary consideration. There is, however, no reason why we should accept this situation, weeping into our Instant Coffee and depriving ourselves of the pleasures a good liqueur has to offer. There is a variety of ways, some demanding patience but all simple and effective, in which we may whip up a whole catalogue of acceptable liqueurs and, as it were, "roll our own", taking the most famous commercial offerings as our inspiration.

In this respect it must be understood that such commercial products as Benedictine, Grand Marnier, Chartreuse and Drambuie, to name but four of many hundreds of liqueurs available, are proprietary products which have, over many years, earned for themselves a well justified and world-wide reputation. The magic of their flavour and fragrance lies in the unique combination of herbs used to aromatise them, the exact evaluation of between thirty and seventy-five different ingredients being conducted behind locked doors.

Under such circumstances it cannot be claimed that any recipe which follows in these pages will produce a liqueur identical to that named as a "type" in the heading that precedes it. It is, however, confidently expected that the final result of any "putting together" along the lines indicated will adequately satisfy the palate of the maker and well justify the small amount of time and expense which the home production of liqueurs entails.

Ren Bellis

Chapter I

The Grass Roots!

LIQUEURS (or "cordials" as they were originally known) are great adventures into strong and special flavours packed with a wallop. Basically they are sweetened spirits or fortified wines richly loaded with the distinctive essences of carefully selected herbs, fruits and flowers, these items in combination being backboned, in terms of degrees-proof, to strengths ranging from about seventeen to fifty-five per cent alcohol by volume according to their type and base. It is, however, worthwhile to mention that not all liqueurs come within this range. There are a number that do not even approach it. "Falernum", for example, is composed of a simple sugar-syrup flavoured with lime, almond, ginger and other spices before being fortified with a small amount of spirit providing a final strength of only six per cent alcohol, whilst "Gomme" has no alcoholic content at all, being merely a strongly flavoured simple syrup.

Most of the "siropes" beloved by the French can be classified as non-alcoholic, their attraction being entirely in the rich flavours they possess. Bearing this in mind, the amateur liqueur-maker may well find it economically worthwhile to experiment with the recipes that follow in later chapters, omitting any fortification by means of spirit. Alternatively, one may pursue a middle way by compounding a liqueur type (Green Chartreuse, perhaps) whilst making such adjustments, in accordance with the Tables on pages 78–84, as will result in a finished product of less strength than the renowned original but one which, in all other respects, remains identifiable.

In these days of breathalyser tests, and having special regard to the fact that alcohol and petrol do not mix, there is, indeed, a considerable amount of commonsense in making such adjustments, and one's ability to convert a 96° proof Green Chartreuse to one of a still significant 42° (the strength of a good

9

commercial Cherry Brandy) without loss of flavour or general benefit of effect is a particular advantage held by the home producer. Those who seek only to produce space-fuel type potables best suited to a witches' dance on a bare mountain can best be left to their own devices.

And what is this "general benefit of effect" a good and sensibly compounded liqueur will provide?

Ask the question of any Frenchman as he sits sipping his cordial: relaxing at some pavement cafe in the glow of boulevard lamps or the setting sun of a Paris evening. He will tell you, briefly, that the effects of his innocent self-indulgence are threefold, providing a sensible and enjoyable way of helping along his digestion, his good humour and, perhaps, his plans for the rest of the night, particularly in relation to the lady of his choice. The word "cordial", you see, stems from the Latin "cordialis" meaning "of the heart ": an association which we should consider further . . .

In the beginning cordials were much sought as love-potions, pick-me-ups, cure-alls and general appeals to the magic of the gods.

Long before Magic had become Science, and when mythology and history danced hand-in-hand, elixirs of a cordial nature were man's last resort and not infrequent comforter. Their origins have no geographical location. Inextricably bound to the story of distillation and the first fermentation of the grape, their start was, above all, universal and without precise setting in time.

Ambrosia, the foodstuff of the Greek gods, was naught more than a semi-solid honey-based liqueur and for many thousands of years the Chinese have cooked up something rather special from the ground bones of the man-eating tiger. The Carthaginians who crossed the Alps to knock their own particular brand of ideas into one of the earliest Roman dictators stopped, occasionally, to swig something reputed to make one of their kind worth three Roman legionaries, and Maecenas always packed a speciality of his own along to the Sabine Farm when visiting his protégé Horace.

Pollio Romulus, a generous man inclined to be more specific than the majority of his contemporaries, spoke enthusiastically to Caesar of a private formulation under the influence of which he contrived to enjoy a full sex-life. He was over one hundred years old at the time and the cynics may, thus, attribute his proud virility to the fact that he also rubbed his aged legs with "oyl", but any schoolboy will tell you that Caesar, who was as bald as a newt, must have had something up his sleeve to make Cleopatra "that way" about him! According to Cicero this could have been a rosepetal distillate and, in this regard, it is worthy of note that Rossoli, a rose cordial, was for many centuries a popular Italian liqueur 'though it is to-day out of favour, having been replaced by Strega, Sambuco and the more sophisticated flavours of international repute.

Whether or not the ancient elixirs really justified their reputations as aphrodisiacs is open to considerable conjecture, and some doubt must attend the reliability of gossip concerning their effectiveness in these directions. Alcohol, Epsom salts or anything else which tends to dissolve the thin veneer behind which our libidos snarl and claw like chained beasts must, if taken over-generously, tend to help raw nature in its natural intent, and it must be remembered that, in the early days of history, the majority of drinking vessels had to be emptied at a draught for, having no base to speak of, they could not be stood upright. Those who might censure the behaviour of the times, when bedroom windows were holes in a stone wall and when even the favourites of the royal courts needed to wear fur-lined panties, should understand that, under those circumstances, a generous shot of the local juice helped all concerned to forget the icicles.

So in spite of the name applied to them, cordials must remain an enigma so far as their vaunted aphrodisiac qualities are concerned, but we can with more certainty identify their less romantic qualities. It has to be acknowledged that the herbs and extracts shuffled together by the medieval alchemists in the universal search for an elixir leading to immortality were no mean choice. Their therapeutic qualities remain beyond question even today. Many of them are still to be found on the pharmacist's shelves, to be measured out into prescriptions supplied by the most modern medicos.

We live in an age of restrictive licence so far as advertising is concerned and, to-day, the commercial producers of our liqueurs do not, and by law cannot, make such extravagant claims as were once a customary part of every sales promotion.

Long gone is the "... summer cordial, acknowledged by the gentry for its remarkable propensity in acting upon the nervous

11

system, the brains and the spinal cord"! But consider the herbs of which we speak: the root of angelica, fragrant, stimulating and having its place in many preparations for the treatment of head colds; the leaves of yarrow, thyme and blackberry, individually serving to reduce temperature, clear flatulence and assist in cases of diarrhoea. Lemon balm, as its name implies, is soothing to the system and, not so many years ago, was widely used as a remedy for hysteria, insomnia and nervous disorders of all kinds. The roots of burdock and bryony still have their place in many a country cupboard (for the clearing of skin and kidney troubles and the curing of coughs and colds) whilst calamus root, with its high lime, sulphur and potassium content, has proved itself an effective stomachic and the relentless foe of colic and dyspepsia.

Our ancestors well knew the pain relieving effects of camomile flower petals, strong scented and bitter, and used them to soothe toothaches, neuralgia and, in the form of a poultice, painful swellings. The astringent lungwort derived its name from the effectiveness of its action against coughs and lung complaints and, less obviously, celery seed has long been regarded as a first line of defence against the rheumatics.

Cardamoms from Bangalore, Mysore or Malabar; cassia bark from India or China; the unripened buds of clove from Zanzibar or, perhaps, the Molucca Islands: all these and a great many more distinguished ingredients have their place and their specific responsibilities in liqueur formulations, the aim of which is not unnecessarily to plunder Nature but to guide her to perfection.

Shakespeare somewhere speaks of "Music like the sweet South that breathes upon a bank of violets, stealing and giving odour". So, too, his pen might have touched, in fantasy, upon the alcoholic vapours which drench, saturate and eventually dismantle flavour and bouquet from the wondrous array of aromatic substances, with their subtle pervasive qualities, which compose to-day's liqueurs: undedicated to any medicinal intent but merely redolent of many mingled and delightful taste sensations.

Not so many years ago, in the days of the old sailing craft, a good few cordials had shipboard origins. These were the "Tart" or "Ship" liqueurs compounded by the ship's barber who, more often than not, additionally served the duties of physician and surgeon. Enthusiasm rather than skill was his primary qualification; bloodletting and plenty of castor-oil were his principal recommendations for everything from headaches to swollen ankles. When, however, patients objected to the enforced application of such treatments, the shrewd consultant spiked the oil with some powerful flavour and added some inspirational alcoholic refinements; the result being a medicinal cordial such as the old Dutch "Hempje ligt op" ... a physic of obvious application since the name can be translated as "Lift up the shirt"!

About the same time, in 1720, a deadly plague ravaged the city of Toulouse, but a small band of crooks, apparently immunized against the disease, moved about unconcernedly plundering the homes of the dead and dying. According to the records, their resistance to the lethal infection was the result of drinking a combination of ". . . the tops of sea and Roman wormwood, a touch of rosemary, sage, mint and rue, two ounces of lavender flowers . . . cinnamon, clove and camphor" in a gallon of wine.

The composite result was called "The Wine Of The Four Thieves", but under any name it would remain recognizable as a homemade liqueur.

We seek our protectives and cure-alls in other forms these days: pills, powders and potions sealed behind plastic barriers and involved conjugate names, but it is doubtful whether any prosaic medicine chest could offer, in comparison with our glass of cordial, so much alleviation from such a variety of ills, spanning the range from sore throats and fevers to kidney ailments and syphilis!

The medieval magic of the old cornucopia-hatted alchemists remains: worked upon, cossetted and refined but, surprisingly, little changed. Tried and proved basic principles cannot be tampered with lightly, but it is inevitable that expertise should have taken the place of inspired dabbling. The putting together of a liqueur has much in common with the composing of a piece of music, each flavour and each nuance of flavour having a parallel in the pitch and duration of a musical sound. Thus even the herbs, masters of the situation from the very beginning, have had to stand up and be counted for grading. There are seven appropriate classifications: strongly aromatic, bitter aromatic, sweet aromatic, peppery, spicy, stimulant and nutty.

Of the strongly aromatic the best known herbs are angelica, balm mint, calamus, caraway, cubebs, juniper, lemon, thyme, orange, lovage, marjoram, peppermint, pimpinella, rosemary and spearmint.

Under the heading of bitter aromatic we can place balm, celery, orris, tansy, elder, guaiac, lavender and sassafras, whilst "peppery" covers capsicum, galanga, ginger, various peppers, white cinnamon and grains of paradise, the pungency of which suggests that "paradise" is a misnomer? In George III's time the storage of these seeds was a serious offence, punishable by a fine of £200!

The spicy aromatics include the familiar cardamoms, cinnamon, cassia, cloves, pimento, mace, nutmeg and vanilla whilst amongst the sweet aromatics are aniseed, carob, coriander, fennel, liquorice and sweet orange.

Cocoa, coffee, tea and cola are not thought of, by the layman, as aromatic substances but so they are, and have their place under the "stimulant" heading, whilst almonds, peach and apricot kernels, tonka beans and woodruff are obvious additions to the "nutty" range, playing a far more important part in the final appreciation of a liqueur than might be imagined. The apricot and cherry, for example, have fruit flavours which might not stir a palate to enthusiasm, but apricot and cherry brandies are quite another matter! The agents of this transformation are the stones included in the formulation, providing the tart, bitter pithiness which so insidiously creeps into the general effect and assists our appreciation of the whole.

The story of Alcohol, the binding spirit, is itself a mystery, having no reliable source.

Note, if you will, the capital "A" used to stress the difference between the .003 per cent of life-essential alcohol (with a small "a") which flows continuously through our veins because of the action of our gastric juices on the starches and sugars we consume (and which, therefore, no group of vegetable-and-grass-juice fanatics, and no authority, can legislate out of existence) and the man-made bonus: the vapourish result of contrived fermentation and distillation. We can but follow the ephemeral fumes of the latter social lubricant a short way along its history, through names like Abou-Mousah-Djafar-Al-Sofi, the Arabian scientist, and Albucasis, the physician of Cordoza. In the term "alcohol" itself (a word of Arabic origin which can, strangely, be translated as "the staining powder") lies our most promising clue.

Those who accept the once popular chronology of the late Archbishop Ussher will tell you that Noah grounded his ark to plant a vineyard, make wine and get drunk a mere fifty generations after The Creation. Archaeologists, who are mean men, disinclined to be as precise as bishops, will merely suck their teeth, shrug their shoulders and make meaningless gestures in the direction of the Mesolithic Age, though the first written mention of winemaking dates only to the reign of Gudea of Mesopotamia, who lived around 2100 B.C. The Pharaohs of Egypt and the kings of Assyria, including Sennacherib and Nebuchadnezzar, certainly braced up when the bottle was being passed round, and vast palace cellars provided a plentiful supply of Instant Gaiety against the possibility of drought. It is not known at which point along the next thousand or so years the processes of vapourization and condensation became knowingly applied, but by the year 800 B.C. the pot was well on the boil in India, where the distillation of flowers had become a firmly established science. Aristotle made reference to the art in 384 B.C., thus anticipating, by nearly eight centuries, the scholarly exposition of the principles and functions of the still given by Zosemus of Alexandria who, incidentally, knew he was a dead duck so far as originality of thought was concerned, freely admitting that he had swiped his ideas from the representation of an alembic (or still) which he had seen in the ornate frieze of an Egyptian temple. The vessel to which he referred was of Arabic design and fulfilled, to a remarkable extent, the requirements of an apparatus intended for alcohol concentration, closely following the chemical principles much later handed on to the alchemists and in use to-day. Its original purpose, however, was the reduction of the mother metal that contained antimony: greatly in demand, as a fine powder, by the eastern flappers of the period who used it, around the eyes, to provide those dark shadows which give our modern misses the appearance of terrified pandas caught in a trap. The word applied to this seductive nonsense was "al kohl" and when it was subsequently found, not necessarily by the Arabs themselves, that the instrument of its production could be put to other and more imaginative uses "al kohl" remained descriptive of the vessel's output.

Towards the end of the Middle Ages there occurred a shift of influence, so far as the health needs of the people were concerned, from the local alchemist to the religious communities, the Brothers of which administered to the bodily needs, as well as the educational and spiritual requirements, of those about them. Great influences were brought to bear by the Church which, through its charitable activities, rapidly established itself as the rock and sure shield to which anyone might go, whatever his or her needs: defence against an aggressor, sustenance or medicine. Inheriting the knowledge and skills of their cordially-minded predecessors, the good friars set to work with a will on the souping up of new and interesting potions. Sometimes sailing into uncharted seas, but dipping and sipping every inch of the way, they steered a course for the wine-merchant's price lists of to-day, in which many of the "Liqueurs Monastique" are still to be found: their rich flavours Flamboyant Gothic and defying all flaw-pickers. These were not born of chance or created of one day's happy dabbling but started, more likely, as an inspiration conceived, perhaps, in the mind of one poetic Cistercian monk and ultimately realised by the work of many.

Along about the year 1510, in the Benedictine abbey at Fecamp, on the Normandy coast of France, a certain friar, himself named Benedict after the founder of his order, brought to perfection the distillation of a sovereign remedy for the cares of the world originally formulated by another: Dom Bernado Vincelli. Over seventy-five different herbs, spices and flowers, including rhubarb root, ginger, centaury, cassia, yellow bugle, angelica, orange peel, masterwort, cardamoms, cloves and vanilla contributed their individual and finely woven magic to the recipe under the persuasion of a fine cognac.

For many years ships of both Dutch and English nationality had been dropping anchor at Le Havre around the time of the grape harvest, filling their holds with brandy from the Cognac district. When the merchants sponsoring such excursions learned of, and had experienced, the Benedictine development, this quickly became an important article of commerce and the future fortunes of the abbey appeared to be set fair for all time. Towards the end of the eighteenth century, however, smoulderings of proletarian discontent, which had long been evident in France, burst to frightening flame. The Bastille, the prison-fortress of Paris, fell to the storming attack of a city mob and at once the whole country became enveloped in the wholesale sacrifice of revolution.

The abbey was closed and its choicest product remained only as a memory to tantalise, but leave unrequited, the taste-buds of those to whom it had once been an experience. Seventy-five years were to pass before the original formula, which had been thought lost, turned up again in a stack of parchment manuscripts being searched by one who was a descendant of the abbey's legal adviser. Manufacture strictly in accordance with the dictates of Brother Benedict's prescription was immediately re-commenced and (God granting some twitchy clown in front of a scanner never gets so excited as to touch the wrong button) seems likely to be inducing its own particular brand of sweet reason for untold centuries yet to come.

Running neck-and-neck with Benedictine in the Popularity Stakes and regarded by many as the Queen of Liqueurs, is Chartreuse: another ancient monastic masterpiece on a most complicated herb base. Cooked up by Carthusian monks in their monastery at Voiron, near Grenoble, and taking its name from the Grande Chartreuse Monastery which cradled its existence in 1607, its initial impact was not so great as that of its rival but when, during the French revolution, its creators were, in common with the Benedictines, banished from their country they had the foresight to pack their formula along with their tooth-brush and returned, twenty-five years later, to carry on the good work in a shed near their original home. With Benedictine temporarily amongst those missing and believed killed, Chartreuse was in an enviable position to be exploited. The Carthusian brothers, who had already proved the assembly of all their marbles, took the situation by the scruff of its neck and shook six bells out of it; distilling, along with their elixir, millions of pounds which went into the expansion of their charitable activities.

When France later divorced church and state a further move was forced upon them but, on the strength of their previous disruptive experience, the monks were equal to the occasion and took themselves off to Tarragona in Spain where they still continue their noble work. For two-hundred-and-fifty years or more the original formulation, based on highly aromatic beds of angelica, balm leaves, hyssop, orange peel and a host of other ingredients, has caressed the senses of succeeding generations, meanwhile achieving all manner of distinctions and becoming available in two different strengths: 96° or 75° proof according to the colour, Green or Yellow, with which our choice is imbued. Individually each distillation has much to offer, 'though the advice of many with erudite and discriminating palates is that both colours should be properly drunk mixed.

A third variety of Chartreuse, white of colour, sometime listed as "Melisse" or "Elixir" and perhaps wistfully remembered as the best of all, has not been made since 1909. We can, however, console ourselves with the thought that, having regard to the legion of liqueurs available (and even whilst you read this, others are being added!) the place of every drop-out is immediately jostled for by a host of near-as-anything calorific contenders. Take, for example the case of Absinthe:

Controversy exists as to its origins, some claiming it to have been the invention of a certain Doctor Ordinaire in the eighteenth century and others referring to it as a fifteenth-century cordial, then made by steeping the leaves of wormwood in equal parts of malmsey wine and thrice-distilled spirit. There can be no such disagreement regarding the potency of its appeal to a large section of the Parisian public in the time of Lautrec and Cezanne, for both painters, in their fondness for capturing on canvas the absinthe drinkers along the Boulevard Malesherbes and in the cafes of Montmartre, left much striking evidence. Faithfully caught by the brush strokes of each masterpiece are the minutest details of the event portrayed, and markedly obvious is the fact that the absinthe drinkers preferred the company of those ladies of the demi-monde who were available. These illicit amours occasioned a multitude of blushes, and when the toxic nature of wormwood was realised the days of absinthe, which depended so mightily upon this bitter herb, were numbered. In many countries, including France, Switzerland and America, it is prohibited and all countries now limit the amount of wormwood which may be added. But does the vacancy remain unfilled? Not at all! Milder substitutes abound. One of the best known is Pernod: Oxygene, made in Belgium, is another. Oyjen (or Ojen) is a dry, well-powered Spanish version.

Take a world map and blindly throw your dart: the point will mark the source of some flavour experience of infinite kilowatts capable of reducing night to an anachronism! Kümmel, distilled from grain and flavoured with the seed of cumin (a plant resembling fennel), originated in the Baltic states under the aegis of Count Peter von Pahlen. Anisette de Bordeaux, one of the "digestive" liqueurs, has been credited to Marie Brizard who is said to have inherited the recipe from a grandmother famous in her neighbourhood for curing the sick. Mexico has made the contribution of Tequila, and from Austria comes Sliwowitz: made of the little red plums that grow on the lower plains. Subrouska is a green vodka from Russia: the Curacaos, which can be white, red or to-day, even blue, are supremely Dutch. To prove that they are capable of more than bourbon and mint juleps the Americans have come up with Creme Yvette, delicately coloured and flavoured with violet, whilst the South Americans have developed Cascarilla, made from spices and barks on a brandy base.

And so on, and so on ... and there you have it: a superabundant international nosegay of scents, colours and flavours with which to drench the tonsils, put muscles on the ego and soothe the inner man.

Generally speaking, liqueurs come just about right: at the end of a meal at the end of a day, and as John Greenleaf Whittier wrote in his *Golden Wedding At Longwood*, "Still, as at Cana's marriage-feast, the best wine is the last".

Home liqueurs can be made more attractive by tasteful presentation: use attractive bottles and labels.

Chapter II

A Matter of Taste

LUCULLUS of ancient Rome, as sly an old rogue as ever darted a cunning glance through forked fingers, had his own liqueur recipe and one completely unrelated to health or pleasure. Particularly designed to serve the interests of beneficiaries-under-wills, bored husbands, jealous lovers and a goodly bag of schemers-in-general it was, at least, succinct. "Take elecampane, the seeds of flowers, vervain and the berries of mistletoe," it read. "Beat them, after being well dried in an oven, into a powder and give it to the party you design upon in a glass of wine and it will work wonderful effect to your advantage."

To-day we seek no special service of our liqueurs, insisting only that they give us pleasure on the basis of their bouquet and flavour, zipped to an appropriate degree by one or other of the compatible hardstuffs.

During the run of our early days, when we were cuddly and fresh-emerged from the skinned poached-egg stage, the decision of what we should drink was taken from us. Mother had everything organised. The drinks were on her and they met our requirements precisely, turning our blotched faces to pink, our squalls to contented gurgles and our fears to nonsense. Now that Milord is considered fully weaned and has expanded his diet in all manner of directions, the responsibility for matching such contentment (or, at least, the hope of finding its near equivalent in a tipple of his choosing) lies squarely upon his own shoulders. His search for the coming time of bliss must be conducted alone. There is no one to advise, for the appreciation or rejection of a particular flavour experience varies from person to person, votes for or against this or that substance being influenced by physiological, psychological and sociological factors.

Surprisingly, whilst there are thousands upon thousands of different smells, there are only four distinct tastes: sour, sweet, salt and bitter, though recent studies have suggested that there are two further well-defined sensations, alkaline and metallic. One might well imagine that such an arrangement of nature would make it comparatively simple for us to decide what we like or what the other fellow would enjoy. Such, however, is not the case for taste, the sense peculiar to the tongue and mouth and the quality in substances discerned by it, is only partly concerned with flavour: a combination of the sensations of both taste and smell. Our reactions to the involved permutations fed to our brain are, thus, the result of rousing influences experienced by two quite separate sensory areas. Taste is detected through the contact of certain soluble compounds (dissolved in the saliva or in the food juices) with the nine-thousand or so taste-buds with which each human tongue is equipped, each bud being set with fifteen to eighteen sensory cells. For anything to provide the sensation of smell, however, it must first vaporise and pass into the nasal cavity where, on portions of the dividing septum, is located the olfactory sensory area on which odour stimuli are received. The exact mechanism is not known. One theory is that the aromatic molecules dissolve in the fluid of the cavity-lining and bathe the sensory cells. Another suggests that the aromatic vapours come into direct contact with the sub-microscopic cell hairs which penetrate the mucus layer: a vast surface area the extent of which may be judged by the fact that in the rabbit some one-hundred-million receptor cells have been shown to exist, each bearing six to twelve hairs!

These two independently motivated sensation areas, the tongue and the nasal cavity, work in conjunction to a quite remarkable extent, the effectiveness of their collaboration being made obvious by a simple practical experiment. Pinch your nose tightly if you will, so that the nostrils are completely closed: then chew on a piece of onion. It will merely taste salt/sweet. Blindfold yourself and repeat the test, having previously talked a friend into feeding you, in varied order, small pieces of onion and apple. You will probably be quite unable to tell them apart. Only when the nostrils are open will the full onion flavour be apparent.

For primitive man, survival frequently depended upon the receptivity of the senses. To-day, although we still possess the basic mechanisms, we no longer use them to the fullest extent except very rarely, sub-consciously, and on those occasions, unknown to most of us, when our bodies are driven by concentration to the very knife-edge of effort. Jackie Stewart, now retired but an undefeated world champion racing driver, will recall one such experience for you. Once, whilst cornering at high speed, he became suddenly aware of a luscious and overpowering aroma of cut grass which momentarily sublimated all other observation. Retracing the track later, on foot, he found that his wheels had merely crushed across the grass verge at that point! With training and experience, however, the senses of taste and smell, the two that principally concern us in the search of cordial contentment, can be redeveloped to an astonishing degree, and the expert can be more precise in his judgement than the finest instrumental technique yet devised. Even so, our appreciation or rejection of a particular compound taste must be an entirely personal matter and, braced ready on the brink of compounding a few flavours for ourself, our best guide must lie in the knowledge of our own likes and dislikes: a knowledge based on experiences which lie in wait, miniaturised for home assessment or, under glass, along the neon-lit, chromed and mirrored shelves of every lounge-bar.

Do not, however, approach your studies with the intellect; relax and enjoy them without a care. Disappointed you will never be, though surprise may well attend your preconception of a flavour hinted by a label. Creme de Cacao, for example, has its beginnings in a sack of cocoa beans, but by the time the distillation of these has been achieved, smoothed and worked upon the liqueur in your glass and the hot chocolate in your mug are of different worlds, the former having a singular and quite unforgettable distinction of its own. Less evocative, but somewhat mind-bending, are the labels bearing names culled by the imaginations of poets and dreamers on flights of fancy: stardust-and-moonlight titles such as Parfait Amour ("Perfect Love") or quaint old Dutch names such as Hansje in de Kelder ("Jack in the Cellar") and Hoe Langer Hoe Liever ("The Longer The Better") or (Heaven preserve us!) Eau de ma Tante!

Fear not at this point, for many are with you, and if you, in your hopeful lifting of the heart, are in need of additional support, we tender it herewith in a selection of notable elixirs representative of liqueur formulations:

ABRICOTINE   A sweet apricot liqueur compounded on the basis of various spirits and fresh or dried fruit together with the crushed kernels which impart a decidedly almond flavour.

ABSINTHE   One of the rarely met do-badders: a potent concoction which became known in France as "La Fée aux oeux verts" (The Green-eyed Fairy) the sale of which is now prohibited in many countries because of the toxic nature of wormwood: a bitter herb occasioning serious nervous disorders but a principal amongst its ingredients which also include angelica, coriander, fennel, anise seeds and cloves.

Following its distillation, Absinthe is coloured with the chlorophyll of nettles or spinach and is then green, but long storage turns its colour to yellow. On the addition of water it becomes opalescent due to the precipitation of certain resins and oils, the same effect being produced by adulteration of the product with gum benzoin as often employed in the commercial manufacture of cheap absinthe.

All countries now limit the quantity of wormwood which may be included in absinthe formulations.

ADVOCAAT   A thick, emulsified, Netherland liqueur mainly composed of the yolks of fresh eggs, aromatic spices, sugar and brandy. This highly commercial and body-building bomb, which is now available in a choice of consistencies, was originally conceived as a home product, principally stemming from farmhouse establishments where hens were always kept. The Dutch farmers, long adept in the distillation of brandy and disinclined to be parsimonious in the matter of its distribution, fortified their yolky home-comfort with enormous but erratic abandon, catching many an unwary drinker unprepared to meet the tongue-loosening charge with which the deceptively smooth buttercup depths were loaded. Of the unfortunate victim suffering an acute attack of verbal diarrhoea people would say "He talks like a lawyer!" and since the word lawyer, in Dutch, is "advocaat" the name was born, but a variety of pseudonyms ("Egg-nog", "Egg-flip", "Egg Brandy" and so on) are extant.

AIREN   A liqueur unusual in its concept, made upon a basis of fermented milk and defying further description.

ALKERMES   A Mediterranean liqueur in which orange-flower extracts are added to the distillate from an infusion of nutmegs,

24

cinnamon, cloves and other less noticeable spices in brandy. The name is also applied to certain types of both French and Italian alcoholic cordials, sweet and usually coloured with cochineal, of indefinite composition.

ALLASCH A very sweet type of Kümmel additionally flavoured with bitter almonds and aniseed (see "Kümmel").

AMBROSIA Originally the name applied to the unbelievably sweet potion of the Olympian gods, reputed to have been a semi-solid honey-based liqueur. The term is sometimes now applied to commercial compositions principally flavoured with vanilla, raspberry and strawberry distillates.

AMER PICON A popular French bitter cordial which is rarely consumed neat but is usually taken as an apéritif in the form of a dilution (two fluid ounces of Amer Picon to about twice the quantity of cold water) sweetened with Grenadine (see "Grenadine").

ANESONE A liqueur strongly flavoured with aniseed and highly recommended to those suffering digestive troubles. A stigma-free alternative to Absinthe, no herb of wormwood being involved in its formulation (see "Absinthe").

ANGELICA A very sweet Spanish liqueur of the Basque region, taking its name from its principal ingredient but additionally flavoured with aromatic plants taken from the Pyrenees.

ANIS A seed liqueur, rather sweet and strongly resembling anisette of which it is a copy, made in Spain or Latin America (see "Anisette").

ANISETTE A sweet and usually green digestive cordial, of French origin, attributed to Marie Brizard, one of the first French women to make distillation her business. Gossip has it that she inherited the formulation from a grandmother who was famous in her neighbourhood for curing the sick, and it is an undisputed fact that Anisette (or "Anisette de Bordeaux" as it may be labelled) possesses tum-settling qualities which recommend its internal application following a meal enjoyed not wisely but too well. Coriander and fennel seeds as well as aniseed provide the flavour, which has been copied and marketted under a variety of names in many different countries.

ANISUM A medicinal liqueur of antiquity, principally flavoured with aniseed, with which Hippocrates, a physician by whose name many a modern medico will swear, is said to have braced up on special but unspecified occasions.

APPLE GIN   A gin-based and colourless liqueur compounded at Leith, in Scotland.

APPLE OF PARADISE   A native of Cuba, being a cordial made from a local fruit.

APRICOT BRANDY   A splendidly rich fruit liqueur having a distinctive "nutty" quality, the agents of which are the crushed kernels permitted to remain during distillation and which impart a fullness of flavour lacking in the fruit itself. Available in a wide range of alcohol strengths (40°–70° proof) according to source.

APRICOT SPIRITS   A general term covering a variety of apricot-flavoured liqueurs, the fortification of which may vary in the nature of the spirit used. Apricot Brandy is, perhaps, the best known, but Apricot Gin, Apricot Vodka and others have their supporters. The fruit used may be fresh or dried and is, in some instances, discarded entirely in favour of artificial essences as based, for example, on Benzyl Butyrate.

APRY   An apricot liqueur: one of the well-known apricot spirits as above.

AMOURETTE   A French liqueur in which lies trapped the flavour and colour of violets. Not a big seller in Australian sheep-farming circles!

AQUA COMPOSITA   One of the most ancient liqueurs, made by macerating various spices and herbs in a wine of high alcohol content.

AQUAVIT   The Danish version of Kümmel, the flavour of carraway seeds predominating (see "Bolskümmel").

ARRAC PUNSCH   The national liqueur of Scandinavia, made by adding a simple syrup and sundry flavours to a base of Batavian Arrack: a somewhat rum-like spirit distilled from rice and molasses which should not be confused with arracs in general, the term "arrac" being used to cover a multitude of sins and a range of crude products prepared from such diverse materials as saps, juices, treacles and mare's milk; one as bad as the other and all producing the effects of a do-it-yourself tonsillectomy.

ATHOL BROSE   A Scot's concoction that is not easily classified and one over the formulation of which the Scotch themselves, imbibers of heroic mould, have been known to wrestle.

"Brose" in the ordinary sense is made by pouring boiling water on oatmeal, the meal knotting. In the preparation of Athol Brose, say some, this preliminary should be followed by the breaking down of the knots and the straining of the cereal liquor. Two parts of whisky and one part of honey are then added, together with a little salt. A well whisked egg and some spices can be further additions. Others claim (and will be damned for it!) that equal quantities of honey and fine oatmeal to which malt whisky is added merely need to be stirred 'till the combination froths when it is ready for bottling, tightly stoppered, for two days' maturing.

AURUM   A rather dry but highly aromatic Italian liqueur, about the colour of pale dry ginger ale.

BADIANE   A liqueur consisting of equal parts of brandy and water with sugar, lemon essence, cinnamon, cloves and almonds added.

BARBADOS LIQUEUR   A West Indian inspiration, principally flavoured with lemon and orange and, more delicately, with mace, cardamoms and cloves.

B. & B.   The happy marriage of Benedictine and brandy.

BENEDICTINE   A sweet, strong and very powerfully aromatised liqueur of amber colour and exceptional reputation which has many times suffered the embarrassment of imitation but which has, for well over four-hundred-and-fifty years, retained its unique position at the head of its class. Its formulation, dating back to 1510 when it was assembled by the good friar Dom Bernado Vincelli and brought to perfection by Friar Benedict in the Benedictine abbey at Fecamp, on the Normandy coast, is said to contain over seventy-five different herbs, spices and flowers including rhubarb root, ginger, centaury, cassia, yellow bugle, angelica, orange peel, masterwort, cardamoms, cloves, and vanilla.

BERNADINE   A herb liqueur based on a monastic recipe dating from the Middle Ages and involving the distillation of alpine plants, selected seeds and a confusion of other exotic, but secret, ingredients.

BLACKBERRY BRANDY   A fruit liqueur based on the fruit from which the name is derived, its flavour being sometimes bolstered by the addition of other fruits and herbs which vary according to its source of manufacture. A small amount of red wine is often incorporated.

BOLSHERWHISK   A well known commercial liqueur, classed as a fruit liqueur, the name of which (part Bols, part Cherry and part Whisky) is actually more contrived than the product itself: a dry blend of cherry brandy and whisky which meet in great harmony and to the satisfaction of all concerned.

BOLSKUMMEL   A Nederland liqueur distilled by Erven Lucas Bols way back in 1575 and claimed as the original upon which all other kümmels are based. The formulation is said to have so impressed a Russian Czar that, following a visit to Holland, he contrived to take the recipe back home with him and eventually made Russia the principal producer and consumer. It is principally flavoured with carraway seeds and cumin, a plant resembling fennel and the source of a highly therapeutic oil. Carraway seeds have been used in various medicinal beverages for more than two-thousand years. The ancient Greeks used them in the preparation of a popular and healthful drink, and in the Book of Isaiah they are mentioned as the basis of a potion that calmed an upset stomach.

BRANDYHUM   A mixture of brandy and Van Der Hum (see "Van Der Hum").

BRUIDSTRANEN   Another name, which may be translated as "Bride's Tears", for the Gold Liqueur, a Nederland composition, once served at fashionable weddings (see "Gold Liqueur").

CALISAY   The national liqueur of Spain, based on a brandy bittered with two-per-cent quinine (a derivative of cinchona) and flavoured with Peruvian bark.

CALORIC PUNSCH   A heart-warming Scandinavian de-shiverer based on sweetened rum and partly named after the elastic fluid that heat was once supposed to be.

CALVADOS   An apple brandy made from the distillation of cider or the pulp of the special small apples which to day grow in the Départmente of France from which the spirit takes its name.

CAPRICORNIA   An Australian liqueur flavoured with various tropical fruits, its name being derived from the Tropic of Capricorn in the vicinity of which the fruits are grown.

CARMELITANO   A Spanish liqueur popular amongst those who enjoy the night-life as well as the sunlight of the Costa Brava. Made by monks of the Carmelite order in Valencia.

CASCARILLA   A liqueur compounded from sundry spices and barks on a brandy base, greatly esteemed by South Americans.

CASSIS   A fruit liqueur in its composition, mainly consisting of sweetened brandy flavoured with black currants, but principally taken in France as an apéritif.

CERASELLA   A cherry brandy made in Italy (see "Cherry Brandy").

CHERRY BOUNCE   An American alcoholic cordial taking its name from the old English term for cherry brandy and usually consisting of brandy, cherry juice, sugar and spices.

CHERRY BRANDY   A richly coloured and flavoured fruit liqueur made by expressing the juice of fully ripened cherries, crushing a proportion of the stones and subsequently distilling. A maturing period usually precedes sweetening by the addition of glycerine and a simple sugar-syrup. Other essences, and further fortification by means of brandy or other spirits, are sometimes employed.

CHERRY HEERING   One of the outstanding cherry-based liqueurs: produced in Copenhagen, Denmark, by the firm of Peter Heering.

CHERRY NALIVKA   A Baltic (and, formerly, a Russian) liqueur which is low in alcohol but of a bright cherry colour.

CHERRY WHISKY   a liqueur made in the fashion of cherry brandy but with whisky as the fortifying spirit. The flavour is most highly esteemed when resulting from the maceration or distillation of black cherries and in some cases small, wild black cherries are employed.

CHESKY   A type of cherry whisky, well-known in Victorian times by the alternative name of "Gean" after the variety of cherry used.

COFFEE RUM   A liqueur the nature and flavour of which are explained by the name. "Tia Maria" and "Kahlua" are typical coffee-rum liqueurs.

COGNAC   A term sometimes indiscriminately applied to all French grape brandies but one which should, more correctly, only be used in connection with the spirit produced around the départements of the Charente and Charente Maritime. Labels carry various signs and letters which are used to distinguish the age of the golden distillate behind them and these may be translated as follows: "Extra"—approximately seventy years old; "V.V.S.O.P."

—approximately forty years old; "V.S.O.P.—twenty to twenty-five years old; "V.S.O."—average fifteen years old; "V.O."—ten years old; "Three Star"—five years old; "Two Star"—four years old, and "One Star"—three years old.

The owner of one of the greatest brandy distilleries in the world was once asked to cross his heart and wish to die in answering the question: how old should the best brandy be? A smile and a twinkle of the eye accompanied the answer "We look upon brandy as a woman, and one does not desire too old a woman!". On the other hand, there is no pleasure to be obtained from a brandy anxious to conceal its youth and irresponsibility behind a flaunting label of doubtful source.

COINTREAU   A colourless liqueur based on fine old cognac distilled with the peel of oranges: one of the group of curaçaos, but one so perfected that it has established a reputation in its own right.

CORDIAL MEDOC   French and a veritable confusion of liqueurs, being a Bordeaux-produced blend of fine brandy, orange curaçao and crème de cacao. Entirely different, but labelled under the same name, is a drink somewhat in the nature of a distilled claret.

CORDIAL REBY   A liqueur with a cognac base, brown in colour.

CRÈME DE ANANAS   A sweet liqueur, also known as "Crème d'Ananas", featuring the flavour of pineapple.

CRÈME DE BANANES   A sweet liqueur based on the flavour of bananas.

CRÈME DE CAFE   A dry, very stimulating and splendidly digestive liqueur flavoured with freshly-roasted coffee beans.

CRÈME DE CACAO   A liqueur popular in France, the flavour and aroma being obtained from cacao and vanilla beans but only remotely related to the chocolate taste one might expect. The word "Chouao" often found on commercial labels indicates that the cacao beans employed were gathered in the Chouao region of Venezuela, considered to be the source of the finest in the world.

CRÈME DE CASSIS   A sweet liqueur having a flavour principally obtained from black currants.

CRÈME DE FRAISES   A sweet liqueur the flavour of which is obtained primarily from strawberries.

CRÈME DE FRAMBOISES A sweet liqueur obtained from raspberries.

CRÈME DE MENTHE A liqueur, distilled in both France and Holland, which may appear in green, white, golden and even ruby guises. The flavour has been libellously described, by some, as reminiscent of chewing-gum but apart from the fact that several varieties of mint, principally peppermint, are included in its formulation, no other similarities are generally evident to the unbiased palate. Balm, cinnamon, ginger, orris and sage are also aromatically involved in the production of this popular cordial which commands a confused stomach with considerable authority.

CRÈME DE MOCCA A sweet seed liqueur, which may be dark or clear, based on the flavour of freshly-roasted coffee beans.

CRÈME DE NOYAUX A liqueur of pronounced bitter-almond flavour obtained from the distillation of fruit stones. A very similar liqueur is known by the name of Persico (see "Persico").

CRÈME DE PECCO A semi-sweet Dutch liqueur, colourless and of a tea flavour.

CRÈME DE ROSE A brandy-based liqueur, very popular in the Gay Nineties, flavoured with the essence of the flower named.

CRÈME DE THÉ A French liqueur unmistakably flavoured with tea.

CRÈME DE VANILLE Classed as a fruit liqueur, the flavour being obtained from vanilla beans.

CRÈME DE VIOLETTE A brandy-based liqueur: another left-over from the 1890's, flavoured with flower essences.

CRÈME YVETTE Somewhat surprisingly an American liqueur, popular in Europe and capturing both the flavour and colour of crystallized violets.

CURACAO Now produced in several countries but initially a Netherlands liqueur dating back to the seventeenth century and made in Amsterdam from gin, sometimes brandy, and the dried peel of small but zestful unripe-green oranges ("Curacao Apples") from the island of Curacao in the Netherlands Antilles where they were first cultivated. To-day, cinnamon, cloves, certain bittering agents and a percentage of Valencia oranges are sometimes added, whilst the use of West Indian brown, in place of white, sugar provides a further flavour variation. Curacaos are presented in a variety of colours (orange, red, green or blue) achieved by the final addition of natural colouring agents.

DAMSON GIN A fruit liqueur prepared on the basis of gin and ripe damsons, some of the stones being crushed and incorporated to improve the flavour.

DANZIG See "Eau de vie de Danzig".

DEMOCKAAT An essentially Dutch blend of advocaat and a full-flavoured mocca made from freshly-roasted coffee beans (see "Advocaat" and "Moccafe").

DICTINE A name applied by a number of manufacturers to a flavour concentrate for the home production of a Benedictine-type liqueur.

DRAMBUIDH An aromatised whisky.

DRAMBUIE Perhaps the best known of all the aromatised liqueurs of its type, being a concentration of venerable Scotch whisky flavoured with heather-honey and a number of herbs which have remained north-of-the-border secrets for many a long year. Said to have originally been the personal liqueur of the Bonnie Prince Charles Edward, who confided it to the Mackinnon family in 1745 in return for services rendered, it has only been commercially available since 1892.

EAU DE VIE DE DANZIG Based on a recipe of Dutch composition which dates back to the seventeenth century, this orange-and-bitters liqueur is to-day made in France as well as in Holland and is, in effect, of the curacao group (see "Curacao"). It has, however, been rendered more elaborate by the addition of minute particles of gold leaf which were originally thought to be a protection against all manner of human ills but which to-day serve no purpose except that they can be swirled and flurried for show purposes (see "Goldwasser de Lachs").

EGG BRANDY See "Advocaat".

ELIXIR A term used somewhat loosely to-day but originally serving to indicate a liqueur of the very highest quality and one possessing definite medicinal virtues. As a name it was particularly applied to a White Chartreuse which once figured prominently in the most selective wine lists but which has not been made since 1909.

ELIXIR D'ANVERS A liqueur very similar to Yellow Chartreuse (see "Yellow Chartreuse").

EŚCUBAC A ratafia made from raisins, liquorice, saffron,

32

cinnamon and other less noticeable spices compounded together in a solution of brandy and water (see "Ratafia").

FALERNUM　A pleasant flavouring syrup, white in colour, composed on a basis of water, sugar, lime, almonds, ginger and other spices. It is fortified to a strength of about 10° proof by the addition of 6% alcohol.

FIORI D'ALPI　A very sweet liqueur flavoured with Alpine flowers and ostentatiously featuring a sugar-encrusted stem in each bottle.

FLADDERAK　A popular Dutch name for a lemon-flavoured gin which has sweetening already added (see "Lemon Gin").

FORBIDDEN FRUIT　A brandy-based American cordial so evocatively named as to have its flavour, frankly citrus and particularly grapefruit, come as an anti-climax.

FRAMBOISE　A raspberry-flavoured liqueur made in Alsace.

FRAISIA　A strawberry-flavoured liqueur.

FRAISE DE BOIS　A liqueur based on the flavour of wild strawberries.

FRIGOLA　A thyme-flavoured liqueur of the Balearic Isles.

GENTIANE　A Swiss liqueur of the bitters type, highly esteemed for its medicinal qualities and based upon extractive matter from a species of gentian.

GILKA KUMMEL　Made in Germany, this liqueur has for a century been accepted as a standard of quality though the long-established firm of Bols in Holland claim that their Bolskummel was the original product. Be that as it may, the flavour is principally obtained from carraway and cumin seed from which is obtained the highly therapeutic cumin oil (see "Bolskummel").

GLAYVA　An aromatised liqueur whisky of a similar type to Drambuie (see "Drambuidh").

GOLD LIQUEUR　A Netherlands herb liqueur distilled from curacao peel and a considerable number of woodland plants, seeds and roots.

In the time of Louis XIV the drinking of "gold" liqueurs actually containing minute particles of the precious metal was a feature at Court and in all aristocratic circles; nor did the habit lessen with the passing of the years, for late into the nineteenth century gold liqueurs were widely drunk along about tea-time. Later still, it became more and more fashionable to serve them at wedding receptions and to this custom Gold Liqueur, still marketed with the flamboyant addition of gold fragments, owes its alternative name of Bruidstranen (see "Bruidstranen").

GOLDWASSER DE LACHS   A brandy-based orange-and-bitters type of liqueur, originally made in Danzig, notable for the fact that it, in common with several cordials stemming from the Middle Ages, contains gold leaf or colloidal gold which the old alchemists believed was good for internal disorders.

GOMME   This is a prepared simple sugar-syrup which may be employed as a base for the carrying of flavours provided by fruit juices or compounded essences. Non-alcoholic.

GRAND MARNIER   Though ostensibly but another of the group known as curacaos this liqueur, based on fine cognac and flavoured with a number of secret herbs which supplement the zest of oranges, has achieved distinction in its own right and is, by many, acclaimed unique.

GREEN CHARTREUSE   Based on a complicated formulation of herbs demanding the addition of angelica, balm leaves, hyssop and a wide variety of other highly aromatic plants, this frankly medieval elixir (first compounded by Carthusian monks of the Grande Chartreuse monastery at Voiron, near Grenoble) is hailed as the Queen of liqueurs by the most contemporary of selective palates: a Queen, one might add, with 96° proof punch tucked up her sleeve!

GREEN CONVENT   A name applied to a French flavouring extract, made at Nantes, for the home production of a liqueur strongly resembling Green Chartreuse.

GRENADINE   A French "sirop" of high density, originally containing a substantial percentage of pomegranate juice but now chiefly prepared by the addition of suitable flavouring extracts to a simple syrup.

GUIGNOLET   A French cherry brandy made at Angers (see "Cherry Brandy").

HALF OM HALF   A Netherlands liqueur, many centuries old, aromatised with angostura bark, the peels of curacao and sweet oranges, cinnamon and cardamoms. The recipe happened by mischance and is said to have been the work of an apprentice who, unenthusiastic at the end of a long day and with thoughts only for the way in which he might spend a pleasurable evening, accidentally transferred a residue of orange curacao into a cask containing stomach bitters. His error remained undisclosed until later when, called upon to fill the glasses with curacao as was the custom of the day, the combined flavours burst upon the taste-buds of his masters with astonishing effect. No record exists as to what happened to the apprentice and one can but hope that he obtained some benefit, and not just a clip across the ear, from a subsequently approved marriage of unlikely partners.

HIPPOCRAS An historically authenticated wine having medicinal virtues, flavoured with various spices and taking its name from Hippocrates, the Greek physician.

HONEY SMOKE A name applied to a commercially prepared flavour-concentrate for the home production of liqueurs in the nature of aromatised whisky (see "Drambuidh").

HYDROMEL A fermented honey and fruit-juice beverage with or without aromatic additions, a large number of variants existing.

IRISH MIST A liqueur consisting of very old pot-still Irish whiskey (spelled, you will note, with an appropriate "e" to differentiate it from the Scots product) flavoured with a few well-chosen herbs and sweetened with Irish heather-honey.

IVA BITTERS Containing gentian, angelica, calamus, coriander, balm, mace and iva herb.

IZZARA A Spanish liqueur from the Basque region, inspired by the much older and better known Chartreuse which it closely resembles, even to the extent of being available in alternative strengths and green or yellow colourings (see "Chartreuse").

JAMBAVA A brandy flavoured by the maceration of plums.

JARCEBINKA A ratafia (see "Ratafia") of Polish origin, made from sorb-apples.

JULEP A sweet spirit-based cordial, almost always flavoured with mint but not to be confused with the long and cool refresher out of Kentucky, of Bourbon or Rye Whiskeys on crushed ice and fresh mint from the garden.

JUNIPER BRANDY A compounded liqueur flavoured with juniper berries.

KAHLUA A rum-based liqueur incorporating the flavour of freshly-roasted coffee beans (see "Coffee Rum").

KERNEL A name applied to a concentrated liqueur-flavouring, redolent of cherry stones and thus applicable to the home production of kirsch-type liqueurs (see "Kirsch").

KIRSCH A cherry liqueur, frequently colourless, of markedly almond flavour since the crushed stones of the fruit are of prime importance in its production.

KIRSCHWASSER A Continental aromatic spirit distilled from the juice and kernels of wild black cherries, a maturing period in glass vessels (a precaution against the possibility of the pure spirit becoming in any way coloured, as it might in vessels of other material) being an essential part of the technique employed in its production.

KIRSEBOER A cherry brandy made in Denmark (see "Cherry Brandy")

KISCHINEFF A Russian liqueur consisting of a spirit tinctured with ginger, mace, aniseed, cloves, balm leaves, calamus and sometimes hops.

KONTUSZOWKA A Polish liqueur flavoured with rose, neroli, coriander, peppermint, lemon, fennel, caraway, wormwood, juniper and aniseed.

KRAAMANIJS An old Dutch liqueur virtually identical with anisette. The name translates to "Confinement Anisette" on account of the fact that, in times past, it was customary for a woman who had just given birth to be treated to a glass of it so that her appetite might be sharpened and her digestion stimulated.

KRAMBAMBULI A liqueur made in the Balkans and based on spirits flavoured with a host of aromatic substances including pimento, cloves, grains of paradise, camomile, galanga, lemon and bitter orange peels, nutmeg and bitter almonds.

KUJAWIAN A highly effective digestive liqueur based on gentian, galanga and bitter orange as the principal agents and with ginger, tonka beans, cassia and pimento as the chief aromatic constituents.

KUMMEL A white liqueur (chiefly flavoured with caraway, orris and cumin: a plant resembling fennel) of which there are Dutch, German and Russian varieties. It is based on a spirit distilled from grain and is especially favoured in the colder countries (see "Bolskümmel" and "Gilka Kümmel").

LEMON GIN Difficult of classification, this can best be described as a "peel drink" since the term "gin" is not really appropriate, merely owing its origin to the fact that in the nineteenth century practically every drink in Holland was called by that name. The recipe was initially inspired by a member of the Bols family of that time who soaked lemon peel in a quantity of genever ("koornwijn" or "grain wine") to produce a result which became known as Schilletje ("Little Peel") or Fladderak. To-day the drink, which may be enjoyed with or without sweetening, is distilled from maize, rye and barley in equal proportions prior to a second distillation with the extremely thin peel of Sicilian Palermo lemons (see "Fladderak" and "Schilletje").

LIQUEUR d'OR Another of the "look-at-me-I'm-dancing" liqueurs, loaded with winking fragments of gold leaf and flavoured with a secret combination of twenty-two different flowers, herbs and seeds.

LINDISFARNE A liqueur whisky distilled and blended to a special formulation on Holy Isle.

LIQUEUR JAUNE The name usually applied to imitations of Yellow Chartreuse (see "Yellow Chartreuse" and "Yellow Convent").

LIQUEUR VERT The name frequently given to imitations of Green Chartreuse (see "Green Chartreuse" and "Green Convent").

MANDARINE A brandy-based liqueur flavoured with small, deep-coloured, mandarin oranges.

MARASCHINO A very sweet Yugoslavian cherry brandy, made at Zadar in Dalmatia, from ripe maraska cherries. A white variety is available and often used in place of sugar or sugar-syrup for the sweetening of compounded drinks.

MARNIQUE An Australian version of Grand Marnier (see "Grand Marnier").

MELISSE A white Chartreuse, sometimes referred to as "Elixir", the production of which ceased in 1909. Recalled by those old-timers who once knew the warmth of its embrace, and who survived the fire and passion of it, as a liqueur of outstanding quality and exceptional alcohol strength.

MELON LIQUEUR A comparatively recent addition to the range of commercially available Netherland liqueurs, based on the flavour and perfume of the ordinary melon.

METAXA A heavy Greek brandy, unique as regards its maturing, since this is carried out in tarred barrels.

METHEGLIN A fermented honey-and-fruit-juice beverage

which may or may not be additionally flavoured with spices, a large number of variants existing.

MIRABELLE An Alsatian liqueur based on a white spirit distilled from the yellow mirabelle plums, of Eastern origin, which were introduced to Lorraine by the Crusaders on their return from Palestine.

MOCCAFE A seed liqueur, dry and possessed of digestive qualities produced from an infusion and percolation of freshly-roasted coffee beans.

MONASTINE A French monastic liqueur, devised at the Abbaye St. Gratien, the flavour of which is reminiscent of, if not identical with, Yellow Chartreuse (see "Yellow Chartreuse").

MONASTIQUE A liqueur blatantly imitating Benedictine and made in South America (see "Benedictine").

MONTE AGUILA A Jamaican rum-based liqueur, flavoured principally with pimento and cloves.

MULBERRY GIN Gin in which mulberries have been macerated for several weeks.

NALEWKA A pleasantly aromatic Polish liqueur flavoured with almonds, cloves and cinnamon.

NOYAU A brandy-based liqueur of pronounced "almond" flavour made from the crushed stones of cherries, peaches, plums and apricots.

ORAGNAC A Netherlands liqueur, dry to the palate, resulting from a blend of curacao and fine cognac (see "Curacao" and "Cognac").

ORANGE BRANDY Brandy in which the peel of oranges, preferably Sevilles, has been macerated for some weeks or even months. The use of orange tinctures for the purpose of supplementing flavour is quite common.

ORANGE GIN Produced by macerating Seville oranges, sometimes with lemons and sweet oranges added, in gin for some weeks. As in the case of orange brandy, flavouring extracts are frequent additions.

ORGEAT A liqueur, which may be alcoholic or non-alcoholic according to taste, consisting of sweet and bitter almond water extract, orange flower water and sometimes a trace of vanilla, the whole being sweetened with sugar. Clarification by means of a suitable fining agent is often necessary and fortification, if

Pottery jugs and other suitable vessels look attractive when merely lettered up. The contents of the corked flagon illustrated have been identified by means of a fibre-tipped pen, the wording being protected by a colourless aerosol varnish spray.

required, is achieved by means of brandy addition.

OXYGENE A Belgian liqueur, markedly flavoured with aniseed but involving a number of herbs which supplement its digestive qualities and encourage its acceptance as a milder substitute for absinthe (see "Absinthe").

OYJEN A dry high-strength liqueur produced in Southern Spain and sometimes called "Ojen" after the town in which it is made. The dried fruits of the star aniseed Illicium verum and other aromatics are used in its formulation, resulting in an absinthe-like flavour (see "Oxygene").

OUZO   A type of anisette made in Greece (see "Anisette").

PALO   A liqueur of the Balearic Isles, flavoured with thyme.

PARFAIT d'AMOUR   A very sweet, violet-coloured liqueur of what has been described as kiss-me-quick flavour, originally developed by the steeping of violets in a clear spirit but to-day of a more complicated base: a mixture of rose, neroli, mace, orange, lemon, almonds, cloves, cinnamon, calamus, cardamoms and rosemary, the cinnamon and calamus predominating.

PASTIS   Another of the multifarious digestive liqueurs bearing a marked resemblance to anisette (see "Anisette").

PEACH BRANDY   A brandy-based liqueur redolent of the fruit named which, in fresh or dried form, is macerated in the spirit along with a proportion of crushed kernels. The addition of a peach flavouring essence to the spirit is an alternative and quite common method of production.

PERNOD   An aniseed-based liqueur, closely resembling absinthe in flavour if not in effect, made in France. Highly recommended for the easing of digestive troubles of all types, two or three glasses sipped during the course of an evening being usually sufficient to have the most obstinate stomach in a submission-hold, patting the mat and screaming for mercy.

PERSICO   A cordial, sometimes spelled as "Persicot" or "Persicoa", based on the combined flavours of cherries, cherry stones, almonds and nuts of all kinds. For more than two-hundred-and-fifty years it has enjoyed a considerable reputation, particularly in England where, in an edition of the *Spectator* dated 17th March, 1712, Addison referred to it in glowing terms.

PIMIENTO   A spicy and effective de-shiverer made on a basis of Jamaican rum flavoured with the essence of the pimento pepper ("allspice") from which it takes its name.

PRUNELLE   An Alsatian liqueur on a brandy base, flavoured with the dark blue fruit and pits of wild plums.

PUNCH   A West Country liqueur made on a basis of combined spirits (brandy and rum) flavoured with limes and various herbs.

QUETSCH   A liqueur (the name of which may appear on labels in the alternative spelling of "Quetch") stemming from Alsace and based upon the flavour of plums macerated in an appropriate spirit.

RABINOWSKA   A pink liqueur the flavour of which is markedly that of rowanberries.

RAKI A Bulgarian liqueur of a flavour well suited to the palate of a man out on a jag; it has a basis of mastic, aniseed and neroli in a mixture of rum, brandy and grain alcohol.

RATAFIA Although often thought of as the name of a specific liqueur, one authority has suggested that all liqueurs owing their flavouring characteristics to an infusion process are ratafias, and that those flavoured during the course of distillation are not. In general, however, the term is applied to any cordial, sweet and alcoholic, the flavour of which is based on nuts, fruits or fruit juices (e.g. Noyau) irrespective of the method employed for its production (see "Noyau").

RED ANISEED One more of the venerable aniseed liqueurs and one particularly popular in the United States, especially well spoken of in Louisiana where it is an old Creole custom to drink it at weddings to that all present might share in the happiness of the bridal couple.

REVERENDINE A very old liqueur of Benedictine type, originally formulated by the Trappist monks of St. Vanne in Lorraine: brothers of an order noted for silence but eager to spread abroad the valuable digestive properties of their elixir.

ROSOGLIO A liqueur of compounded spirits flavoured with cloves, angelica, almonds, cinnamon, neroli and rose.

ROSTOPSCHIN A liqueur of very strong aniseed flavour additionally aromatised with cloves, cinnamon, coriander, sweet orange and lemon.

SCHILLETJE A Dutch name, meaning "Little Peel", for a Netherlands lemon-gin with sweetness already added (see "Fladderak" and "Lemon Gin").

SHRUB A very old, and once very popular, drink compounded of rum and lemon-juice which, taken hot and with sugar added, becomes to-day's Rum Toddy: a thing of beauty and of unassailable reputation, even amongst teetotallers, for curing, or at least making more pleasant, a cold in the head.

SILBERWASSER A Danzig-type liqueur in which small particles of silver are incorporated, silver being once considered a cure-all addition in the Middle Ages (see "Eau de vie de Danzig").

SKY CREAM A dry compounded herb liqueur the principal ingredients of which are mature Scotch whisky and a carefully balanced herb distillate sweetened with honey.

SLIVOVITZ A Yugoslav plum-brandy (which may also be styled "Slivovica", "Sljivovica" or "Sliwowitz") known for at least seven centuries and of international reputation. Particularly large and sweet plums of the pozega variety are used, no tree being cropped for the spirit until it is at least twenty years old. A proportion of the crushed fruit kernels are used for the purpose of introducing their slightly bitter taste to the final product which, when additionally flavoured by means of juniper berries, becomes a further type of plum-brandy known as "Klevovaca".

SLOE GIN First compounded in England from a wild plum known as the sloe or blackthorn berry, sloe gin is a preparation of gin flavoured with sloes either by simple maceration or maceration and distillation. It is usually sweetened with sugar-syrup and is frequently improved by the addition of almonds or crushed fruit kernels during the period of its flavour development.

STREGA A strong and sweet Italian herb liqueur, strongly flavoured with the zest of oranges. The word strega means "witch": beware, therefore, the bewitching effect!

TIA MARIA A coffee-rum liqueur (see "Coffee Rum").

TRIPLE SEC A liqueur in the form of a re-styled curacao: colourless, higher powered and less sweet (see "Curacao").

VAN DER HUM A sweet liqueur based on an old Netherlands recipe but one made in South Africa, by the Cloete family, for over two-hundred years during which time it has been adapted to feature the peel of "naartjes" or Cape oranges. Cinnamon, cloves, nutmeg, cardamoms and orange blossoms are additional ingredients, all of which are macerated in a brandy spiced with a percentage of rum.

The name "Van der Hum" was coined in South Africa by the original Dutch immigrant who could not recall the name of the liqueur's first discoverer, and therefore applied the equivalent of "Mr. What's-his-name".

VIEILLE CURE Another version of Green Chartreuse (see "Green Chartreuse").

VISNEY A Turkish cherry-brandy, once popular in England and quoted, in the wine merchant's price lists of 1773, at £1.0.0d per gallon!

WHITE CHARTREUSE See "Melisse".

YELLOW CHARTREUSE The "other", only slightly less

famous, product of La Grande Chartreuse monastery, in no way degraded by its reduced alcohol content and switch of colour from green. Based on a similar type of complicated herb formulation as its respected opposite, there are many who claim that the two liqueurs, Green and Yellow Chartreuse, make excellent marriage partners which can only be appreciated to the full when combined in one glass: a point of view expressed by the jovial friar who, asked to define true happiness, replied "One part Green and two parts Yellow". (see "Green Chartreuse").

YELLOW CONVENT   A name applied to a French flavouring extract, made at Nantes, for the home production of a liqueur resembling Yellow Chartreuse.

YULAN   A compounded spirit in which magnolia flowers have been steeped, or to which magnolia essences have been added. Petit-Grain, an essential oil distilled from the leaves and twigs of bitter and sweet orange trees, tangerine peel and bergamot are usual additions.

ZEER OUDE GENEVER   The oldest type of genever gin, distilled from maize, rye and barley in equal proportions and spiked with juniper berries.

ZOMBIE   A West Indian liqueur of the corpse-reviver type. To its composition go as many different types of rum as can be assembled plus sugar-syrup, apricot liqueur, pineapple juice and lime juice, all ingredients being shaken and strained (as are the customers!).

ZUBROWSKA   A Russian spirit of the vodka type in which zubrowska grass has been steeped to provide colour, bitterness and a slight aroma.

The poets amongst us might invest with romance a warm June evening heavy with the breath of red roses. Breath of red roses nothing! The dedicated chemist will recognise it as the complex whiff of geraniol, citronellol, citral, eugenol, linalol, nerol, and various alcohols and aldehydes.

Chapter III

Getting the Strength

SEVERAL times during the course of each year, in countries all over the world, well-tailored elder sons of elder sons exchange their trim jackets for aprons, take up shovels and retire behind locked doors to shuffle into place several-hundred-pound loads of spices and herbs assembled strictly in accordance with memorised formulae. Then come standard procedures of liqueur production: distillation, infusion, maceration, the combining and balancing of different flavours by simple addition, or a combination of two or more of these methods according to the nature of the ingredients involved.

The very finest liqueurs are undoubtedly produced by the distillation process. Carefully assembled aromatic and flavouring constituents are initially steeped in a suitable wine or spirit which is then vaporized under close temperature control, condensed in accordance with the most exacting conditions, left to stand for a week or so before being coloured (or de-colourised) as required, and filtered or "fined" prior to being aged in oak casks. Our great-great-grandmamas may well have operated their own private stills, on a similar if less scientific basis, as a routine part of their housewifely duties. Well into the seventeenth century a still (or "Limbeck" as it was then known) formed a major part of the accepted domestic arrangements, and even to-day ('though the derivation of the word may be questionable) a still-room remains the housekeeper's particular province in every large establishment.

From between the gently browned and crisping pages of old books come recipes designed to provide the young bride with (and I quote) "all the vertuous illustrations meete for her knowledge" so that she might "then sort her mind to the understanding of other housewifely secrets, right profitable and meete for her to use, such as the want thereof may trouble her when need or time requires".

For the preparation of Aqua Composita, for instance, she would "take Rosemary, Time, Issop, Sage, Fennell, Nip, and roots of Elicampane of each a handful, or Marjoram and Penny-royall of each half a handful, eight slips of Red Mint, halfe a pound of Licoras, halfe a pound of Aniseeds and two gallons of the best Ale that can be brewed."

The instruction continues: "Wash all these hearbs clean and put into the Ale, Licoras, Aniseeds and hearbs. Put into a clean brass pot and set your Limbeck thereon, and paste it round about that no Ayre come out, then distill the water with a gentle fire, and keep the Limbeck cool above, not suffering it to run too fast and take heed when your water changeth colour to put another glass under, and keep the first water for it is most precious, and the latter water keep by itself, and put it into your next pot and that shall make it much better."

Such routines, however, are not for us!

Since alcohol boils at 78° centigrade and water (constituting eight to nine parts of all wine) at the much higher temperature of 100° centigrade, the distillation process would seem to be a simple one to apply.

Such is not the case.

Alcohol, the natural product of fermentation, is composed of not one but many substances, scientifically containing one or more hydroxl groups classified as "primary", "secondary" and "tertiary". Ethyl alcohol, unless indulged to excess (an exercise which may be described as putting the quart before the hearse) is innocent enough, for this is the grape or grain spirit which helps build friendly acquaintance, thaws commercial ice and has its place in civilised society. Regrettably, however, poisons in the form of Methyl ("wood") alcohol and other higher alcohols constituting Fusel-oil also result from the fermentation process, and 'though these represent no health hazard if left to themselves in their normally insignificant quantities they do, under conditions when enthusiasm and ignorance dance hand-in-hand, concentrate to a draught of pure disaster. The toxically-induced traumas of America's shame carnival of the 1920's, when bathtub gin was brewed in defiance of Prohibition and hooch liquor, smelling of vinegarised gunsmoke, was "aged" with floor-wax, remain on record in the blind and mental institutions, as well as the cemeteries, of that country.

The admonition "Thou shalt not" in relation to the process of do-it-yourself distillation (or, for that matter, any other method of alcohol concentration as, for instance, deep-freezing) is not always accepted as a commonsense proposition. To some it is, and will always remain, a challenge to be met with rebel songs. Wispy puffs of illicit smoke rising from back of small sheds in quiet corners of the Emerald Isle, particularly at week-ends when the local representative of law-and-order has his feet up, sometimes foretell great times ahead for certain inhabitants of a Little Bit of Heaven. One cannot, however, avoid the suspicion that those who tend the pots are playing a wary game, the dangers of which have greater consequence than the crunch of an Exciseman's boots upon the gravel. We are wise to turn away from such temptations and stand forthright at our "local", paying for our degrees-proof according to the alcohol strengths we seek. And it should be noted, in passing, that the separation of alcohol by freezing is every bit as illegal as distillation.

"Proof" – the magic strength – means 57.06% alcohol by British reckoning. Prior to the invention of the hydrometer by a certain Exciseman name of Sikes it was measured, in this country, by a lunatic system involving a pile of gunpowder soaked with a sample of the liquor under test. A match was applied to the damp mass and if the result was a steady flame the liquor was "proved". A weaker mixture either refused to co-operate or merely smouldered; a stronger one frequently led to a nasty conflagration.

To-day, of course, we have a precise definition of the term, firmly stated in Officialese and set out as follows: "Spirits shall be deemed to be proof if the volume of the ethyl alcohol contained therein made up to the volume of the spirits with distilled water has a weight equal to that of twelve-thirteenths of a volume of distilled water equal to the volume of spirits, the volume of each liquid being computed as at 51°Fa."

Translated to plain English this means that "100° proof" on a label indicates the presence of 57.06% alcohol by volume or 48.24% alcohol by weight.

The Continentals, on the other hand, measure strength in terms of alcohol by volume only, the figure being prettily expressed as so many degrees Gay-Lussac: thus 100° on a French label means 100% alcohol. To further confuse the matter, U.S. proof, like the

American gallon, is just a little smaller. Whereas absolute alcohol is 175.1° British Proof, it is 200° U.S. proof. In short, the Americans simply double the Gay-Lussac figure, leading many an unwary label-shopper from these shores into anticipations of promises never fulfilled. No doubt they have their reasons.

To convert British degrees-proof to percentage alcohol by volume (for all but the most precise calculations demanding several places of decimals) one multiplies by four and divides by seven as in the following example:

70° proof × 4 = 280. Then 280 ÷ 7 = 40. Thus 70° proof = 40% alcohol by volume.

Comparative scales: wine and spirit strengths

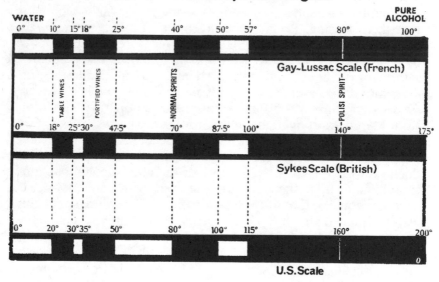

The following Table of Comparisons, compiled on this basis and covering the range of particular interest to the home liqueur-maker, is adequately appropriate:

| Degrees = | % Alc. by Vol | Degrees = | % Alc. by Vol | Degrees = | % Alc. by Vol | Degrees = | % Alc. by Vol |
proof		proof		proof		proof	
33	18.9	60	34.3	87	49.7	114	65.1
34	19.4	61	34.9	88	50.1	115	65.7
35	20.0	62	35.4	89	50.9	116	66.3
36	20.6	63	36.0	90	51.4	117	66.8
37	21.1	64	36.6	91	52.0	118	67.4
38	21.7	65	37.1	92	52.6	119	68.0
39	22.3	66	37.7	93	53.1	120	68.6
40	22.9	67	38.3	94	53.7	121	69.1
41	23.4	68	38.9	95	54.3	122	69.7
42	24.0	69	39.4	96	54.9	123	70.3
43	24.6	70	40.0	97	55.4	124	70.9
44	25.1	71	40.6	98	56.0	125	71.4
45	25.7	72	41.1	99	56.6	126	72.0
46	26.3	73	41.7	100	57.1	127	72.6
47	26.9	74	42.3	101	57.7	128	73.1
48	27.4	75	42.9	102	58.3	129	73.7
49	28.0	76	43.4	103	58.9	130	74.3
50	28.6	77	44.0	104	59.4	131	74.9
51	29.1	78	44.6	105	60.0	132	75.4
52	29.7	79	45.1	106	60.6	133	76.0
53	30.3	80	45.7	107	61.1	134	76.6
54	30.9	81	46.3	108	61.7	135	77.1
55	31.4	82	46.9	109	62.3	136	77.7
56	32.0	83	47.4	110	62.9	137	78.3
57	32.6	84	48.0	111	63.4	138	78.9
58	33.1	85	48.6	112	64.0	139	79.4
59	33.7	86	49.1	113	64.6	140	80.0

Any vegetable matter which contains sufficient starch or sugar, be it the sap of a cactus plant or the contents of a Tate & Lyle syrup tin, can be (and has been) used as the basic material of spirit production. The coddled and cossetted spirits suited to our civilised purpose fall, however, within two general classes: those made from potato or grain starch, distilled to a fairly high proof and purified and filtered 'till of an almost neutral nature (retaining little or no flavour of their own) and those such as whisky, brandy, rum and so on which are easily identified by the palate.

Of the former the best known is Vodka, usually bottled at around 68° proof and well suited to the stimulation of liqueurs within the 40°–54° proof category. That is not to say Vodka cannot be used for liqueurs normally of much higher alcohol content. If, however, we intend that our home-made product should draw as closely as possible to the known commercial offering, then a strict adherence to the latter's strength is important. In this connection the following guide in respect of some commercial masterpieces and their strengths will be of service:

ANISETTE		44 degrees proof
APRICOT BRANDY	40–70	”	”
BENEDICTINE	73	”	”
BLACKBERRY BRANDY	55	”	”
CHERRY BRANDY	42	”	”
COINTREAU	70	”	”
CREME DE ANANAS	44	”	”
CREME DE BANANES	52	”	”
CREME DE CACAO	47	”	”
CREME DE MENTHE	52	”	”
CURACAO	52–70	”	”
DRAMBUIE	70	”	”
GOLDWASSER	70	”	”
GRAND MARNIER	67	”	”
GREEN CHARTREUSE	96	”	”
IRISH MIST	70	”	”
KUMMEL	68	”	”
MARASCHINO	55	”	”
PEACH BRANDY	40–70	”	”
SLIVOVITZ	70–87	”	”
SLOE GIN	45	”	”
SOUTHERN COMFORT	88	”	”
STREGA	70	”	”
TIA MARIA	55	”	”
YELLOW CHARTREUSE	75	”	”

It will be appreciated that the use of a 68° proof spirit added to a combination of sugar-syrup, flavourings and other ingredients, no matter how generously employed, can never achieve more than a percentage of the original strength of the spirit itself. If, then, our sights are set on the putting together of a liqueur such as Cointreau at 70° proof we are obliged to employ, for its fortification, a neutral but essentially alcoholic additive well beyond the final strength at which we aim and one capable, so to speak, of raising our syrup-flavour concoction to eminence by its boot straps.

Such a liquor is Polish Spirit, which should be easily obtainable from any good wine merchant (who will be glad to order it for you if it is not already on his shelves) in 13 fl. oz. half-bottle quantities. Deceptively colourless and virtually taste-free, this is a spirit to dominate any situation, being 80% alcohol by volume and packing a 140° proof punch. Since it is priced not on its actual value but on the basis of a tax proportionately adjusted to its strength it may, during that first tooth-sucking moment when someone hands you the bill, seem an expense to be avoided if possible. Further consideration will lead you, however, to the realisation that it serves the purpose of more than twice its volume of any other spirit and so can prove a marked economy in the long run: a point well illustrated by a comparison of the Alcohol Strength Adjustment Table provided later in this chapter.

The more flavoursome spirits of which we have already spoken (and there are those folk for whom the unique contributions of whisky, brandy, rum and gin will always have a special attraction: their hearts being behind such familiar labels, just below the cork) can, of course, be employed for fortification purposes within the degrees-proof limit imposed by the spirit itself. In this connection the commercially available liqueur flavourings, which can be purchased from most home-winemaking supply stores in small and moderately priced quantities, offer a wide variety of interesting possibilities when used in combination with the various types of spirit open to selection. With whisky, for example, try Reverendine, Dictine, Cream of Apricot, Cream of Mirabelle, Cherry Brandy, Cream of Cacao, Curacao, Yellow or Green Convent, Mandarine, Peach, Prunelle or Honey Smoke. The flavour of brandy marries well with Cream of Apricot, Cream of Green Mint, Cream of Mirabelle, Cream of Cacao, Cherry

Brandy, Yellow Convent, Green Convent, Peach, Prunelle or Curacao, whilst those intent upon stiffening the situation by means of gin should try (if only for the sake of their digestion) Cream of Green or White Mint, Yellow or Green Convent, Curacao, Danzig, Kummel or Anisette.

Rum is equally adaptable and open to experiment but has obvious uses in the production of all coffee-based liqueurs, winter warmers and fog-cutters in general, served with or without a pillow for each customer.

Whichever spirit is used, it is far too expensive a commodity to be splashed about indiscriminately. Fortification is something to be approached with circumspection and reverence for the assembled flavours, sweeteners and strengtheners that await their mingling. The addition of the spirit of our choice is an exercise aimed at the achievement of a reasonably precise ingredient balance.

The Alcohol Strength Adjustment Table "A" that follows is designed to assist this worthy purpose. In all cases, the volume occupied by an adequate quantity of sweetening matter has been allowed for. This (standardised as 4 oz. of sugar per 26 fl. oz. bottle) accounts for the difference between the additions recommended in Column A (parts of an *unsweetened* solution) and those of Column B (parts of the same solution *after* incorporating the necessary sugar).

Put to service in accordance with the examples provided, the Table will be found of use in the putting together of many fruit brandies, gins, and liqueurs (e.g. Coffee Rum) of precise alcohol impact. Because it quotes additions in terms of "parts" rather than fluid ounces, cubic centimetres, millilitres or any such nonsense, its application is equally suited to the production of a bottleful (26 fl. oz.) or a mere 26 cc. tasting sample for the stimulation of further activity. In the latter case, however, it has to be presumed that a syrup constructed to the specifications of Column A (so many parts of basic solution or fruit juice plus 4 oz. sugar) has already been prepared for addition in accordance with the recommendations of Column B.

The liqueur strengths covered have, in all cases, been rounded off to their nearest meaningful whole-figure measure.

ALCOHOL STRENGTH ADJUSTMENT TABLE "A"

Parts: Basic non-alcoholic solution/fruit juice (in all cases needing to be sweetened by standard addition of 4 oz. sugar) per bottle.	Parts: Basic non-alcoholic syrup resulting from 4 oz. sugar addition to previously unsweetened solution/fruit juice.	Parts of Spirit Added — Degrees Proof				Resulting Strength of Liqueur
		68	70	80	140	
A	B	C	D	E	F	G
13½	16	—	—	10	—	31° proof
11½	14	12	—	—	—	31° proof
11½	14	—	12	—	—	32° proof
17½	20	—	—	—	6	32° proof
12½	15	—	—	11	—	34° proof
10½	13	13	—	—	—	34° proof
10½	13	—	13	—	—	35° proof
17	19½	—	—	—	6½	35° proof
11½	14	—	—	12	—	37° proof
9½	12	14	—	—	—	37° proof
9½	12	—	14	—	—	38° proof
16½	19	—	—	—	7	38° proof
8½	11	15	—	—	—	39° proof
10½	13	—	—	13	—	40° proof
8½	11	—	15	—	—	40° proof
16	18½	—	—	—	7½	40° proof
7½	10	16	—	—	—	42° proof
9½	12	—	—	14	—	43° proof
7½	10	—	16	—	—	43° proof
15½	18	—	—	—	8	43° proof
6½	9	17	—	—	—	45° proof
6½	9	—	17	—	—	46° proof
8½	11	—	—	15	—	46° proof
15	17½	—	—	—	8½	46° proof
5½	8	18	—	—	—	47° proof
5½	8	—	18	—	—	49° proof
7½	10	—	—	16	—	49° proof
14½	17	—	—	—	9	49° proof
4½	7	19	—	—	—	50° proof
4½	7	—	19	—	—	51° proof
14	16½	—	—	—	9½	51° proof
3½	6	20	—	—	—	52° proof
6½	9	—	—	17	—	52° proof
3½	6	—	20	—	—	54° proof
13½	16	—	—	—	10	54° proof
2½	5	21	—	—	—	55° proof
5½	8	—	—	18	—	55° proof
2½	5	—	21	—	—	57° proof
13	15½	—	—	—	10½	57° proof
4½	7	—	—	19	—	59° proof

Parts: Basic non-alcoholic solution/fruit juice (in all cases needing to be sweetened by standard addition of 4 oz. sugar) per bottle.	Parts: Basic non-alcoholic syrup resulting from 4 oz. sugar addition to previously unsweetened solution/fruit juice.	Parts of Spirit Added — Degrees Proof				Resulting Strength of Liqueur
		68	70	80	140	
A	B	C	D	E	F	G
12½	15	—	—	—	11	59° proof
3½	6	—	—	20	—	62° proof
12	14½	—	—	—	11½	62° proof
2½	5	—	—	21	—	65° proof
11½	14	—	—	—	12	65° proof
11	13½	—	—	—	12½	67° proof
10½	13	—	—	—	13	70° proof
10	12½	—	—	—	13½	73° proof
9½	12	—	—	—	14	75° proof
9	11½	—	—	—	14½	78° proof
8½	11	—	—	—	15	81° proof
8	10½	—	—	—	15½	84° proof
7½	10	—	—	—	16	86° proof
7	9½	—	—	—	16½	89° proof
6½	9	—	—	—	17	92° proof
6	8½	—	—	—	17½	94° proof
5½	8	—	—	—	18	97° proof

The Table can be used in a variety of ways to meet the needs of different situations. The following examples will illustrate this point:

1. It is desired to produce a 26 fl. oz. quantity of a Coffee Rum liqueur (combining freshly-made coffee, 4 oz. sugar and 80° proof rum) having a final strength of 34° proof. How should the three ingredients be balanced?

Method: Locate the required strength in Column G. Tracing this back to Column A it will be found that 12½ fl. oz. of coffee will be needed. These, sweetened by the addition of 4 oz. sugar, will provide 15 fl. oz. syrup as per Column B (*Note:* Since 4 oz. dissolved sugar occupies a volume equivalent to 2½ fl. oz. of liquor, no further adjustment should be necessary). This amount of syrup, fortified with 11 fl. oz. of rum, will provide the strength sought.

2. A standard Coffee Rum recipe calls for 8 oz. of sugar to be dissolved in 9 fl. oz. of hot coffee, the resulting syrup being fortified with 12 fl. oz. of 80° proof rum to provide a final strength of 37° proof. What alteration need be made to the formulation for the production of a brandy-based liqueur of similar strength?

Method: Reference to the Table reveals that a final strength of 37° proof is not obtainable by the use of 70° proof brandy. It is, however, closely matched by the 38° proof figure. Tracing this back to Column B, 12 fl. oz. of coffee syrup are indicated. The amount of sugar involved in this instance is, however, double the standard 4 oz. addition and will occupy a volume equivalent to 5 fl. oz. of liquor. The Column B figure must, therefore, be corrected (by subtraction of the sugar's volume equivalent) to read 7 fl. oz. This quantity of coffee, sweetened with 8 oz. of sugar and fortified with 14 fl. oz. of brandy, will provide the liqueur required.

3. Prior to embarking upon quantity production of the 34° Coffee Rum liqueur as calculated in Example No. 1 it is intended to produce a 26 cc. sample for tasting purposes.

Method: Following the Table's requirements exactly as before, dissolve 4 oz. of sugar in 12½ fl. oz. of freshly-made coffee. Use a measure calibrated in cubic centimetres to draw off 15 cc. of the resultant syrup and combine these with 11 cc. of 80° proof rum.

The balance of syrup need not be wasted but can be transferred to a sterilised and appropriately sized screw-cap bottle fitted with a cork for extra protection. This, set across two short lengths of wood at the bottom of a saucepan, is immersed in water to the level of its shoulder. Very slowly the water is brought to a simmering temperature of 83°–88° Centigrade (181°–190° Fahrenheit) and maintained thus for twenty minutes, at the end of which time the bottle, placed on a thickness of newspaper or a wooden surface, is allowed to cool. The cork, when dry, is trimmed as necessary, painted with a thin coat of melted paraffin-wax, and capped with the bottle's screw-on closure.

Syrups so treated may be stored over a prolonged period for use as required, and make a useful contribution to the liqueur-maker's range of easily accessible flavourings for experimental addition in the development of new formulations.

The application of Table "A" is limited to the fortification of solutions completely lacking any alcohol content of their own. To this extent it serves well enough in the case of liqueurs largely based on traditional country recipes. These stem from days when Spirit Duty amounted to no more than a few shillings per gallon (it was only 11s. 0d. at the birth of the present century!). They do not, therefore, make any concession in respect of ways and means of cost-cutting, as, for instance, by the incorporation of a substantial quantity of alcohol which we may, without restriction of licence, produce for ourselves.

The entirely natural process of fermentation, capable of converting a maximum three-and-a-half pounds weight of sugar to around eighteen per cent alcohol by volume in a gallon of liquor, is ours to command. It can make a big contribution to the economy of liqueur making, an idea extensively explored in the next chapter.

All the necessary ingredients for a swift putting-together of a superior acquaintance-rigger! (see next chapter).
From left to right: a wine of not-too-definite flavour, Polish Spirit, sugar (best added in the form of a syrup) and commercially available flavourings to suit one's inclination. Those shown here are concentrates produced under the brand names of T'Noirot, Winemaster, Bertolini, Bush Boake Allan and E. F. Langdale.

Chapter IV

Getting the Strength—But Cutting the Cost

ABOUT a third of the desired strength of your liqueurs can probably be obtained from your own home-made wine, the rest must come from added spirit.

As far back as the history of our subject records, wine has been an accepted vehicle for the bringing together of all the qualities a liqueur should, by definition, have to offer. Almost any wine will serve for this purpose and, strangely (since under all other circumstances they would constitute an embarrassment), the very dullest and most uninteresting ordinaires are the best of all for us to use. Expense is, thus, no barrier to their generous employment, and the cheapest commercial products (probably of table strength, around 21° proof and so labelled) can also be pressed into use if necessary.

Most liqueurs can be made from the white and darkly golden home-made or commercial wines, since taste-free vegetable colourings can always be introduced to meet specific requirements. In this regard, however, it must be emphasised that the colour of a liqueur is a matter solely for the concern of the purist, the degree of licence permissible being well illustrated by the availability of red, white and even blue curacaos and the popularity of Creme-de-Menthes that may be white or pink as opposed to the more familiar green.

Red wines are not so adaptable, though obviously well suited, particularly when of the full-bodied port type, to the needs of liqueurs such as cherry and other fruit-based brandies demanding to be appropriately pigmented.

Formulations intended to be of a markedly significant flavour (curacaos, for example, in which the zest of oranges is the predominant agent) will obviously receive a worthwhile headstart by being based upon an orange wine, but in general, wines of too strong a flavour should be avoided unless the totally new experience of their combination with some contrasting additive is deliberately sought.

What the amateur liqueur-maker needs is a cheaply produced, clear-as-water, virtually taste-free but strongly alcoholic solution which he may subsequently colour, flavour, sweeten and further fortify to whatever extent he wishes.

Prevented as we are, by law and common-sense, from distilling or concentrating alcohol, we can quite legally produce it by the process of fermentation, and therein lies the answer to many problems.

There are many good reasons for putting the phenomenon to work for us: and only one reason for not doing so, the idea that it, like the mating of elephants, involves a procedure likely to be above one's head. In point of fact (as the man said when congratulated on the birth of a son) there is really nothing to it! Nature, like mama, does the work, and it is merely our responsibility to ensure that Nature, like mama, gets a fair chance.

The agent of the fermentation miracle is yeast: a microscopic single-celled plant, about one five-thousandth of an inch in diameter, which is of the vegetable kingdom, entirely dependent upon chemical energy derived from the digestion of food synthesised in the form of sugar from other plants.

Classified as "budding fungi" on account of the way in which they reproduce themselves, yeasts are more variable as regards shape, quality and potential than the assembled flowers of any garden. Related species can be numbered in their hundreds, the family having what amounts to a universal distribution. The bloom of fruits, the nectar of blossoms, the husks of grain and the surface of all living things have their invisible but substantial hordes. An acre of typical farm soil, taken to a depth of only six inches, holds about one-hundred pounds weight of apiculates (the general term by which wild yeasts are known) and they have been detected at heights up to 35,000 feet. We cannot, without effort, escape their influence, and it is understandable that the yeasts themselves, crowded together in such diversity that several species may exist side by side on the same leaf or berry, refuse to be intimidated by their neighbours, preferring to pull up the drawbridge and live independent existences.

An actual and painstaking count, taken in a wine-growing

district of America, revealed that the waxy bloom of a single grape harboured about one hundred thousand moulds, an equal number of wine yeasts and more than ten-million other yeasts of mixed variety lumped together under the apiculate classification. Had the area been newly planted with vines, or never used for the growing of grapes, the moulds and undesirable wild yeasts would have been the sole residents.

At the dawn of history, before magic had been turned to science and Man was still spending the greater part of each day propitiating and conciliating the gods against what was likely to happen to him on the morrow, it was generally believed that good and evil spirits hovered over every brew and decided the result, which might vary from fair to stinko, according to which were the stronger.

Substitute the words "desirable wine yeast and apiculates" for "good and evil spirits" and it will be seen that the curious practices of the Ancients touched upon a glimmer of truth.

Much later, as the world grew a little, it became the ambition of the medieval alchemists to penetrate the fermentation mystery. They instinctively felt that, once this mystery was solved, the way for further important discoveries in biology and medicine would be opened to them. It was, however, left for Van Leeuwenhoek, at the end of the seventeenth century, to be the first to study yeast cells through a microscope, and many more years were to pass before Louis Pasteur broke through the chaos of previous beliefs by proving the indispensability of yeast to the fermentation process. He it was who fairly placed the responsibility for poor brews of low alcohol content, frequently laced with off-flavours, upon the wild yeasts which dominated the majority of situations, and it was whilst looking for a way in which the true wine yeast minority might be guarded against the intrusion of such elements that he developed his theory of pasteurization.

To-day, in commercial laboratories, wineries and breweries all over the world, sealed phials lie resting in little tiled cells, under lock and key. These contain pure yeast cultures covering every possible brewing requirement. Included in their number are superlative specimens collected from the finest grapes of the best vineyards, for it has been ascertained that they carry in their chromosomes certain characteristics of the soil from which they originated, of the climate in which they thrived, and of the vines upon which they lived. These characteristics, responsible for the famous names of wines with "Appellation of Origin", will be passed on, for the ultimate benefit of both professional and amateur users, via daughters further persuaded from these exemplary captives, for each concern is proud of its yeast's family tree and takes every precaution to ensure that its ward may continue to lead a normal, happy life without care and away from disturbing influences.

True wine yeast cultures, available under many brand names and representative of every well-known type, may be purchased from any winemakers' supply store for the matter of a few pence. In the form of dried granules or tablets individually sealed under an inert gas, as dormant sediments at the base of sterile solutions contained in miniaturised test-tubes and as communities sealed from contamination on sloping beds of nutrient agar jelly, these quiescent cells merely await the right environment in order to achieve the purposes we have in mind for them: purposes that will, of course, dictate our selection.

In the making of liqueurs, our essential need is for alcohol: lots of it or, at least, as much as we can get. Since various yeasts have different potentials in this respect, some being able to tolerate higher concentrations of alcohol than others, our choice must be for one of a true Sherry type capable of surviving in strengths up to 32° proof and, we may hope, having its origins on the small, sweet Palomino grape grown in the white calciferous soil natural to the finest Spanish vineyards. Pause, however, before you release it to do your bidding. Remember all the care taken to ensure the purity of the product, the benefits of which can quickly be negatived by carelessness in subsequent handling.

In the air about us, on our hands and every item of equipment we intend to use, are innumerable millions of rapidly multiplying wild yeast spores and acetic bacteria of all types. Consider, then, what happens should we allow these to intrude upon our production process:

The fermentation will start surely enough, entirely under the influence of the wild yeasts present. They, by sheer weight of numbers, will dominate the situation and remain the masters of it for about twenty-four hours. Since, however, they are but poor fermenters, only able to act upon simple sugars and thus prevented from making use of sucrose in the form of the Household Granulated we may have provided, only a low yield of alcohol results. On the other hand, a high percentage of unwanted acids, injurious to our cause, will have developed as a result of their activity.

Twelve hours later they are finished. A solution of about 4% alcohol swirls about them and at that concentration they die or, to be more exact, indulge in a form of self-destruction: then a phenomenon known as autolysis takes place and can be responsible for the development of the most unpleasant off-flavours. Meanwhile, of course, the founding parents of our sherry yeast colony have been putting up the stockades and indulging in a population explosion with which to man them. The unleashed off-flavours and the unsolicited acids are, however, already present.

Fortunately, our defences against the intrusion of unwanted yeasts and bacteria are simple, effective and easily applied.

An insistence upon visual cleanliness can be taken for granted. In this connection it should be noted that CHLORIDE, in the form of an ordinary domestic bleach, serves well in the preparation of very dirty jars. A solution made up of one part bleach to nine parts of water is appropriate, but it's use must always be followed by a most thorough rinsing. The slightest trace of chloride entering into our subsequent plans will cause the development of the most foul off-flavours. In this regard (and particularly during hot weather) some small but not to be ignored threat of chloride contamination exists in the water piped to our homes. Alert local authorities, whose first consideration must obviously be the delivery of a bacteria-free supply for drinking purposes, will oftimes increase the chloride content at source; sometimes to a point at which it actually registers on the palate. It is, thus, advisable to regard all water as suspect and to use only that which has been boiled and allowed to cool. Even more effective is the use of an antichlor: usually a substance of a sulphite nature.

POTASSIUM METABISULPHITE, most conveniently handled when compressed and packaged under the name of Campden or Fruit Preserving tablets, and SODIUM METABISULPHITE (best employed as a stock solution: 2 oz. of the crystalline salt made up to 20 fl. oz. with water and clearly labelled for use as required) are both reliable antichlors and either may be used in that capacity.

The amount of sulphite needing to be employed is infinitesimal. One cupful of water to which has been added a single campden tablet (or one teaspoon of sodium metabisulphite stock solution) will provide an effective final rinse for all vessels and equipment cleaned by the use of bleach, and one teaspoon of the same dilution may, with complete confidence, be directly added to each gallon of water actually used in the putting-together of any recipe, adequately serving to remove any traces of chloride which may be suspected in the local supply.

With everything visually beyond reproach, there yet remains the necessity of dealing with the apiculates already spoken of and ganged against us on every surface.

Although some of the microbes present may be highly resistant to destruction (the spores of some bacteria are able to survive many hours of boiling in water and can withstand chemical treatment for an equally long period) none of those menacing our project is immune to a thorough drenching with sulphur dioxide: a pungent gas which, over many years, has served the winemaker and brewer well. For its most convenient source of supply we turn again to the sulphite compounds already mentioned. Both of these release considerable quantities of the gas when dissolved in water to which a little CITRIC or TARTARIC acid has been added. The result is a solution which, for general sterilising purposes, should be swilled round our jars and sponged over every single item of equipment. No further rinsing is necessary. Everything may simply be left to drain before use since any drops of the solution remaining upon them, and finding their way into our fermentation, will do no harm. We shall indeed find, as we proceed, that the deliberate addition of a small amount of sulphite to our ingredients is a recommended step.

Sterility is like Virginity; there are no half-measures. You either have it or you have not! So, in the preparation of a sterilising medium, it pays to ensure that maximum effectiveness will be achieved.

Eight Campden tablets (or their equivalent: 1 fl. oz. of a previously prepared sodium metabisulphite stock solution) incorporated with 10 fl. oz. of water to which a level-teaspoon of either citric or tartaric acid have been added will do their job magnificently. Solutions so prepared have, however, a time-related efficiency. They should, therefore, be made up as required and discarded at the end of each session.

Nutrient salts are to yeast what K-rations are to the soldier on active service: a readily accessible and conveniently packaged supply of get-up-and-go!

Yeast is a plant, and it needs to be provided, particularly when first launched, with nitrogen, potassium and phosphorus exactly as does any plant in the garden except that, whereas the keen horticulturist may satisfy demand by the simple expedient of stretching a hand to the nearest compost heap, we are obliged to seek a more salubrious source.

There are many excellent proprietary compounds available in both powder and tablet form. These adequately provide the three stimulant influences necessary to ensure our yeast making a good start. Alternatively, you may prefer to try your hand at a little economic sorcery by purchasing the basic ingredients and mixing your own. To this end the following will prove a useful guide:

AMMONIUM PHOSPHATE   Of all the compounds commonly referred to as "yeast nutrient salts" this is the most helpful since it supplies both the nitrogen and the phosphorus necessary to ensure a strong ferment. Its introduction to an alcohol-producing formulation also serves to keep to an acceptable minimum the quantity of higher alcohols likely to otherwise develop (see page 113). One heaped teaspoonful added to every gallon of must (the name by which we know our assemblage prior to and during the early stages of its fermentation) is a worthwhile routine.

POTASSIUM PHOSPHATE Supplies both potassium and phosphorus and can be helpful in the reduction of excess acidity: half a level-teaspoon per gallon of must is, therefore, a recommended addition.

MAGNESIUM SULPHATE   Not at all necessary in hard-water districts (where the piped supply will normally contain an adequate quantity) but a useful additive in those areas where the water is naturally soft. Only a pinch per gallon, mark you, for magnesium sulphate, by any other name, is Epsom Salts and can provide a service you don't expect.

Finally, whilst at your mysteries, slip a Vitamin B_1 tablet (or, more prosaically, half-a-teaspoon of Marmite) into the pot for the encouragement of cell growth and, in consequence, a more rapid ferment. Used during the later stages of alcohol development – perhaps to re-energise a ferment not proceeding as strongly as it should – a further Vitamin B_1 addition will often prove helpful in achieving a resumption of full activity, but on such an occasion use only one-half, or even one-quarter, of the tablet since any large amount left in solution and not metabolised by the yeast can give rise to a characteristic taste.

The time has now come for emphasis to be placed upon the fact that, in the channelling of our thoughts towards the cost-reduction of liqueur fortifications, we are not concerned with wine-making as such. Though we tread a parallel path to the winemaker over much of our journey, his and our objectives differ.

He is concerned with the development of flavour and bouquet: balance and body. We are not.

The product *he* seeks is an end in itself (requiring only the prescribed addition of one jug, one loaf of bread and a Thou, blonde or brunette, to comprise paradise).

Our need is simply alcohol. Our choice of a suitable basic ingredient is limited to the common cereals, and of these rice is the one best suited to our purpose. Four ounces only: just enough to stuff a milk pudding, go round a curry or throw at a wedding!

The use of rice for the production of alcohol dates way back to at least 700 A.D. Rice-fermented Saké, a name abbreviated from the Japanese words "sakae-mizu" meaning "prosperity water", has long been the national acquaintance-rigger of Japan, and the Chinese have lushed up something similar under the name of Samshu.

Unfortunately, wine yeasts cannot directly ferment carbohydrates in the form of starch: not because their tiny cells lack the necessary chemistry, but because the starch molecule itself is too large to be absorbed through the membrane that forms the cell wall. Since the yeast only possesses the necessary means of accomplishing starch decomposition within itself, some supplementary outside influence needs to be brought to bear. Then, with the starch molecules already on their way to becoming an amenable source of sugar, the yeast is able to take control of the sequence of events to follow.

The outside influence referred to is an enzyme: one of a considerable group comprising the Gentle Persuaders of the invisible world of constant chemical change.

Enzymes are busybodies with an Interferiority Complex. Defiantly resisting all attempts on the part of those who would expose their complex structure, little is known of them except that they are secreted by micro-organisms and will, under conditions approved by them, act vigorously to promote a reaction between one substance and another without themselves being changed. They are stimulated by temperatures up to 65° centigrade but become inactive beyond this point, eventually suffering complete devastation. They can usually tolerate antiseptics and are as essential a biological need as the necessity of being able to sort the lads from the lasses. Our bodies contain them in abundance, and were we to be deprived of their function our entire digestive system would cease to exist. The moment we put food into our mouths an enzyme known as Ptyalin shrugs off the covers and gets to work on the job of converting our victuals to virtues. Present in saliva, its purpose is to help change our starch intake to the sugars dextrin and maltose, and since it demands either a neutral or slightly alkaline medium in which to work its miracles, it only retires from the contest after we have swallowed and the food has arrived in our stomach where acid gastric juices are present. From that moment on two further enzymes, Pepsin and Rennin, take over.

In the very earliest days of alcohol production from rice grain the natives of the Far Eastern countries had an unaccountable awareness of the part played by ptyalin in the breakdown of the starch molecule and assisted their fermentation programme by sitting around, group chewing and spitting the grains into a communal tub: a practice that still exists amongst certain remote tribes. Much later, in the face of a more hygienic approach, it was discovered that a further enzyme, named Diastase by the two French chemists who succeeded in isolating it, was also capable of producing maltose from starch, the maltose being open to subsequent conversion to fermentable glucose by means of maltase. Since then a considerable range of enzymic products for starch saccharification have reached the amateur market, one of the best known being AMYLASE: a stock line so far as most retailers are concerned. This, or some such, we should have by us when the time for toe-tapping is over and the serious business of getting down to it is due to commence: a moment upon the verge of which we stand, for only one major contributor to the strength we seek remains to be discussed.

The term "sugar", to the layman, means only the white granulated, cubed or slightly moist brown stuff by means of which he cushions the impact of other palate experiences and plays hell with the calories. In point of fact, a remarkably wide range of closely related substances come under the same heading and are, by the chemist, classified and subdivided into extensive lists of precise names with which, except for three, we have no concern.

"Sucrose" is sugar as we buy it: the familiar product we so quickly locate, and queue so long to pay for, at our Self Service. White Household Granulated is our mark since demerara, brown and other such, quite apart from being more expensive, are less pure and will induce colour and flavours we would rather avoid.

Not entirely unknown to yeasts in their natural surroundings (plums, for example, contain a high proportion of it and peaches depend upon it almost entirely for their sweetness) sucrose does, however, present certain problems so far as yeasts are concerned. Their appetites are for the sugars "fructose" and "glucose", and it is just a fortuitous stroke of chemical good fortune that the arrangement of carbon, hydrogen and oxygen elements that compose sucrose can be disentangled by the chemistry of the voracious cells and re-assembled in two groups providing fructose and glucose respectively. This "inversion" of the original order of things has supplied science with the name "Invertase" for the enzyme that achieves it, and us with the term "Invert" descriptive of the two new sugars, in combination, that result.

The time taken for the re-arrangement of the three elements to be completed, though it may be measured in hours rather than days, nevertheless applies a brake to the start of fermentation proper. So it is to our own interest to speed things up as far as possible by doing a little sucrose inverting on our own account, thus leaving the yeast free to concentrate on the more important matters in hand.

The process by which we induce the inversion of sucrose, by chemical rather than enzymic means, is easy to follow.

66

Preparing the sugar-syrup. The quantity required (5 fl. oz. per 26 fl. oz. bottle) is easily made by dissolving 4 oz. of sugar in 2½ oz. of water under the influence of gentle heat and continuous stirring.

Put 4 lb. of ordinary household sugar (sucrose, that is, in our new understanding) into a large pan with one-pint of water and a short half-teaspoonful of either citric or tartaric acid. Heat this mixture until it boils, stirring frequently until all the sugar crystals initially settled at the bottom of the vessel have dissolved. Continue to boil gently for half-an-hour or so (during which time the syrup will acquire a very pale straw colour): then allow to cool and add whatever water is needed to produce a total volume of exactly four pints, each pint of which will contain one-pound exactly of now inverted sugar.

Bottled and labelled for use as required, precise step-by-step addition of invert sugar may, thus, be made in accordance with the following scale of equivalents:

Fluid ounces of prepared syrup		Weight of invert sugar (oz.)
20	=	16
17½	=	14
15	=	12
12½	=	10
10	=	8
7½	=	6
5	=	4
2½	=	2
1¼	=	1

The syrup offers two additional advantages over and above the inversion of our recipe's necessary sugar-ration. Firstly, it enables us to make the introduction in liquid (and therefore easily involved) rather than solid form (which bugs the susceptibilities of the yeast no little!), and secondly it makes simple whatever calculations are required to ensure that, when all things are assembled down to the last ounce, the sum total of our product amounts to exactly one gallon. Yeast does not, under the

The syrup should, under no circumstances, be allowed to boil, a simmering being all that is required.

circumstances for which it was biologically designed, have to square up to the exceptionally high concentrations of sugar such as we intend to thrust upon it. We can anticipate its reaction to our large-scale plans by putting ourselves, figuratively speaking, in its place: seated at table and served with every single item of an extensive menu, from hors d'oeuvre to cheese and biscuits, on one brimming, swimming, totally revolting plate. We should not, I feel, get far beyond our napkin; yet if the very same items, in exactly similar portions, are fed to us bit by bit at discreet intervals we can wolf the lot and still find the desire, when only the crumbs remain, to reach for the nuts or the lady of the house according to our inclinations.

Accept this comparison as a means of assessing the yeast-sugar relationship and you will appreciate the extent to which we can assist the fermentation process, and minimise the risk of its coming to a sudden halt, by adopting a "sugar-by-stages" technique. When making these successive additions in the dry straight-from-the-packet form, however, it is far too easy to forget the increased bulk of the final product induced by each contribution. Eventually we run out of jar space with further sugar still needing to be added. Actually knowing the *volume* a full sugar complement will occupy, and being thus able to leave sufficient room for it, no such problem arises.

But enough of dissertation. We stand upon the threshold of practical experience, with nothing to prove but proof itself: the higher the better. And here is how we set about it, starting with the collecting together of all the items required to take our project through from tentative start to triumphant conclusion and only excluding such items as small pans, bowls, measures, spoons, funnels and other things which come easily to hand in most households:

EQUIPMENT (1) Two one-gallon glass jars (one as a spare for switching purposes) fitted with corks or rubber bungs bored to take the stem of an air-lock. Similar vessels made of unpigmented, odour-free and non-toxic plastic would be a second choice since these do not so easily reveal their inner workings and most people like to see their yeasts slaving for them. Old stoneware jars, which may be lead-glazed, and metal containers of all types (unless they be of stainless steel throughout) should be avoided at all cost since these, contacted by a fermenting liquor, can produce truly poisonous results.

(2) A glass or plastic air-lock: not merely an elaborate device for keeping the flies out of our business but a very practical winemaking aid the purpose of which is to act as a spur to drive the yeast the way we want it to go. In order to understand this function it is necessary to appreciate that the cells, in pursuance of their expansionist programme, need the energy that oxygen provides. If oxygen is freely available to them as air they need seek it from no other source. In consequence, the pampered darlings are inclined to loll like profligate sultans: budding merrily but making little or no contribution to the urgent needs of mankind.

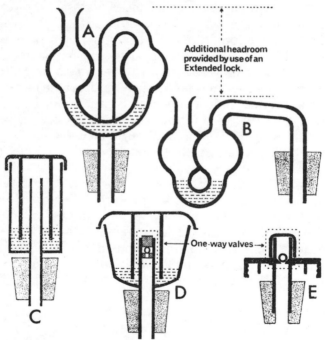

SOME COMMONLY MET-WITH TYPES OF AIR-LOCK

A: *"Conventional" pattern, available in either glass or plastic.*
B: *"Extended" pattern, made of glass, particularly recommended for use when headroom is limited.*
C: *Plastic "Handy" lock, available in alternative sizes.*
D: *"Vinty" special plastic air-lock, fitted with a one-way pressure valve which enables it to be used with or without water content.*
E: *Plastic "Sentry" dry lock (Pat. app. for) operating on the rise and fall of a small bearing.*

70

If, however, we cut off the air supply available to them they are obliged to turn to the sugar we have provided for the energy they need and, in so turning, split the sugar two ways: half to carbon dioxide gas and half to the alcohol we intend for our future enjoyment.

The gas, as much as one-hundred litres of it from only one pound of sugar, has to be liberated if the build-up of its pressure is not to blast sudden and unscheduled release in a disastrous confusion of shattered hopes and flying glass. Hence the need of an air-lock, operating on a half-inch or so of water or the rise and fall of a small bearing according to type, which permits the escape of fermentation-induced carbon dioxide whilst preventing the ingress of air.

(3) A four-foot length of rubber or plastic tubing, preferably fitted with some simple sediment-avoiding device (such as a foot or so of glass tubing bent to a J-shape, a piece of rigid plastic tubing punched with a ring of small holes at a distance of half-an-inch or so from a plugged end, or any one of several gadgets now commercially available) for the transfer, by siphoning, of liquor from one vessel to another.

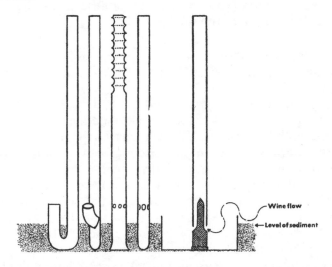

Five different types of sediment-avoiding siphon bottoms (made of either glass or plastic) in general use. The term "J-Tube" (though obviously applicable to the conventional pattern seen extreme left) is frequently employed to identify fitments of other shape but, as will be seen from the diagram, all serve the identical purpose of allowing a wine to be siphoned from one vessel to another without disturbance of yeast deposit.

Ingredients
1 dessertspoon: pure malt extract
4 oz. long-grain rice
3½ pints: invert-sugar syrup
Half a level-teaspoon of grape tannin *or* one tablespoon of really strong cold tea
Nutrient salts
1 Vitamin B_1 tablet
Amylase enzyme
Citric acid
1 Campden ("Fruit Preserving") tablet
Sherry yeast

Of all these items, the one most likely to raise a surprised eyebrow is the strong cold tea. Regarded by some as a minor additive its presence is, in fact, of major importance. The tannin it introduces plays a vital role in preventing the development of off-flavours, in extending the keeping qualities of the brew under construction, and (since it combines with and precipitates those substances which tend to promote and stabilise hazes) in aiding the eventual clarification of the final product.

Method By way of overture to all that follows we prepare something universally accepted as a Yeast Starter Bottle. And here's why:

In its quiescent state as purchased yeast, if directly added to any sort of properly assembled fermentable medium, will for a long time apparently do nothing. The calm, as it happens, is misleading! In secret, because of their microscopic size, generations upon generations of buds are gradually stirring to activity with a dedication of purpose that would do credit to a saint posing for stained glass. Since, however, each single fluid ounce of our brew needs to contain upwards of six-thousand-million healthy cells before the show is fully open to the public, the cells before the show is fully open to the public, the establishment of a propagating station (a well aerated, yeast-flattering environment of limited and controllable volume) is a first step in the right direction. Here the yeast may be persuaded to develop an adequate colony in much less time than would otherwise be necessary.

Pausing, then, only to remember the importance of having all equipment clean and sterile, pour half-a-pint of water on to one dessertspoonful of pure malt extract, two tablespoons of a previously prepared invert-sugar syrup, a level teaspoon of citric acid and a measure of proprietary nutrient salts as recommended by its manufacturer *or* a saltspoonful each of ammonium and potassium phosphate.

After stirring well to ensure that all the ingredients are properly involved, with no heavy malt layer at the bottom of the pan, bring the lot to a boil and allow to simmer for two or three minutes. Then, when the solution is quite cold, transfer it to a well rinsed bottle which should be shaken for the deliberate aeration of its contents immediately prior to the addition of a Vitamin B_1 tablet, the tablespoon of strong cold tea, and the sherry yeast.

With its neck stoppered by means of a cotton-wool plug, the bottle should now be placed in a warm atmosphere (the spare corner of an airing-cupboard is ideal) or any controlled temperature not exceeding 80°F. Meanwhile, during the pause necessitated by our having to wait for the hot starter solution to cool, we can proceed with one other preliminary to our project: the enzymic disintegration of the starch molecules we intend to wring. This merely involves boiling our four ounces of rice in one pint of water for exactly (but *exactly!*) five minutes. The entire slop of grains and moisture is then switched to a sizeable bowl of minimum half-gallon capacity and, when cool, given the addition of one crushed Campden tablet plus a level teaspoon or so of Amylase or whichever starch-reducing product is available.

Covered with a clean towel, the bowl and its contents now need to be left – again in a warm atmosphere – for 48-hours during which time the contents of our starter should have come to full activity. Should this convenient balance of events be not achieved, no harm will come from waiting upon the yeast a little longer.

The combining of all we have achieved so far and a first addition of sugar in any volume constitutes the third step of our production routine: i.e. the contents of the now lively starter-bottle are added to the rice-grain mixture together with half-a-pint of invert-sugar syrup, one teaspoonful of citric acid and (unless some proprietary nutrient is being used) one heaped teaspoonful of ammonium phosphate plus half a level-teaspoon of potassium phosphate.

Again covered and returned to the beneficent warmth previously provided, the rice pulp will soon be in a vigorous ferment. At this point it needs to be strained through a piece of linen (sterilised, of course, by being boiled or sulphited and subsequently rinsed) into a one-gallon jar, firm hand pressure being applied 'till all the moisture has been extracted and only a solid mass of spent grains is left behind.

Approximately two pints of liquor will result from these attentions, and the addition of a further two pints of invert-sugar syrup, followed by three pints of cold boiled water, should now be made. Then, after everything has been swirled together to ensure a proper involvement, all air is excluded from the fermentation vessel by the fitting of an air-lock. From now on a surrounding temperature of 65°–70°F. is sufficient and should not be exceeded.

An energetic passage of tiny bubbles up the sides of the jar, visible through the translucence of its contents, will initially be matched by an almost continuous activity of the lock. As the weeks pass, however, the excitement will gradually diminish 'till hardly any movement may be distinguished. From this point (by which time a considerable deposit of exhausted yeast cells will have formed, in peaks and raised ridges, across the bottom of the jar) we need to feed the no less powerfully-operative survivors with one pint more of the invert sugar prepared for them. This should not, however, be fed all at one time but in continually decreasing quantities: ten fluid ounces with then a pause for renewed activity: five ounces, then two-and-a-half and so on until the limit of the yeast's alcohol tolerance is achieved.

At around 18% alcohol by volume (32° in terms of proof) the contents of the jar will begin to clear. The liquor should then be siphoned off its deposit into a replacement vessel and adjusted to exactly a one-gallon quantity by the addition of whatever cold boiled water is necessary. Thus released from the restrictive influence of the alcohol strength that brought it to a halt, the yeast may now proceed to act further upon any sugar that remains. A further period under lock is, therefore, necessary. By a speeded rejection of suspended solids the liquor may, on the other hand, continue to clarify: a final indication that all things possible have been achieved and a situation calling for its continued transfer from one vessel to another (a procedure known as "racking") whenever a build-up of sediment becomes evident.

When all is as clear as spring water, two crushed Campden tablets dissolved in a little of the product and added to the bulk immediately prior to bottling (properly corked spirit bottles, labelled not as wine but "Liqueur Wine Base", are appropriate to the occasion) will serve to protect any residual sugar from attack by occasionally lurking lactic-acid bacterium. This would be an unlikely event under all the circumstances, but to be forewarned is to be forearmed and we have not journeyed as far as this to be thwarted in our success (that chemical compound of man with moment) by a bug!

Since all liqueur formulators are, by the very nature of their activities, self-confessed optimists (convinced that all peas are sweetpeas, that all houseflies are looking for a way to get out, and that all bottles are half-full when they are, in fact, half-empty) it is unbecoming that too much stress should be placed on the possibility of things going amiss. This can, however, happen and it is as well that we should be prepared to apply remedial action when necessary. The worst and most frustrating eventuality that could occur would be the halting of our sugar-to-alcohol conversion before the full potential of the yeast is realised, and the complete cessation of all activity in the jar (at a time when substantial quantities of the syrup remain to be introduced) would lead to a situation needing to be faced. A diagnosis of the possible cause of the disaster, and the application of remedies suggested by the following trouble-checking chart, should, however, put matters right.

One final point: whilst you are waiting for your base wine to finish fermenting, use cheap commercial wines for your liqueur-making. Apply what patience you can before pressing your home-produced social lubricant into service.

It is not easy to idle your motor when you feel like stripping your gears, and many newcomers to the fermentation process, separated by nought more than a cork from lots of lovely wassail, will find it irksome, if not impossible, to accept that alcohol, in any form and of whatever concentration, continues to improve 'till out of its short pants and on the way to sophistication. That, however, is how things are, and the matter is brought to your attention since you needs must know the rules before you break them.

Our liqueur wine-base, like any liquor, is better in its usage than in its telling, and in the recipe section of this volume there are enough formulae to keep the widest-ranging palate cavorting forever in the fields of rice.

For the moment, then, (whilst waiting upon nature to plod its course), uncork a bottle of some unassuming commercial stuff, select a spirit suited to your intentions, and riff through the pages that follow to an oasis of refreshment headed "For Instant Enjoyment". There you will find an assemblage of encouragements specifically designed for the whiling away of dragging time. Whatever your choice of flavour, whatever your choice of spirit, whatever your choice of supplementary benefit in the form of shop-bought wine or personally produced base, the Alcohol Strength Adjustment Tables "B", "C" and "D" that follow will guide you through to a product of any final strength within the range of 37° to 98° proof. By their comparison with the Table "A" of chapter three the economies they have to offer will be at once apparent.

In all cases allowance has been made for the inclusion of an appropriate amount of sweetening syrup to meet the needs of the average palate. The quantity required (5 fl. oz. per 26 fl. oz. bottle) is easily made by dissolving 4 oz. of sugar in 2½ fl. oz. of water under the influence of gentle heat and continuous stirring. A greater volume can, of course, be produced by adjusting the amounts of sugar and water proportionately. Similarly, the standard syrup addition may be reduced or increased to suit individual requirements, in which case a re-assessment of the liqueur's final strength needs to be made on the basis of a mathematical formula provided amongst the appendices to this volume.

Check	Possible cause	Diagnosis	Action to be taken
1.	Temperature too low.	The great majority of modern wine yeasts are able to continue their activities down to 42°F. Every degree reduction of temperature does, however, impose a restraint upon them and, in the case of cells already reduced in vigour by an accumulating strength of alcohol, the fermentation process may be brought to a halt.	Transfer the fermentation jar to a warmer atmosphere, the final stages of the fermentation process being best conducted in an atmosphere of 75°–80°F.
2.	Yeast colony out of balance.	During the initial vigorous fermentation period of the liquor, when a considerable amount of dissolved oxygen still remains accessible to the yeast, the very rapid development of new cells far exceeds the number suffering exhaustion. When, however, the available oxygen has been used, and the colony is dependent upon the sugar provided, the ratio of live to dead cells is reversed 'till, under normal conditions, a satisfactory balance, commensurate with the prevailing conditions, is attained. If, however, the increasing alcohol yield, and the restriction it brings to bear, is such as to place too great a burden on cells already working to the limit of their capabilities, then the entire process is at risk of being brought to a premature conclusion.	(a) Remove air-lock and splash liquor in order to reaerate. If no result: (b) Add a further teaspoonful of ammonium phosphate and half a level-teaspoon of potassium phosphate plus one quarter to one half of a Vitamin B₁ tablet according to how close the true end of the fermentation cycle is.
3.	Temperature of liquor too high.	Although a temperature of 75°–80°F. is suited to the atmosphere surrounding a starter-bottle, and the third stage of the process detailed, it must be understood that the energy of a fully active yeast colony in bulk will itself produce heat. Under these circumstances it is not unknown for a fermenting liquor to have been left at around 78°F. and then to have crept well beyond 80°F. under the impulse of its own action, the yeast being thus devastated before fermentation was complete.	Move the fermentation vessel to some slightly cooler spot. The probability is that a fresh sherry yeast will need to be introduced. This is best added in the form of a further starter, made to the original pattern. When this is fully active it should be made up to double its volume by an addition of the inactive bulk liquor. Then, when these composites are together in full ferment, their quantity is again doubled, and so on until full fermentation is once more achieved.

ALCOHOL STRENGTH ADJUSTMENT TABLE "B"
(applicable to the use of 21° proof (or 12% alc. by vol.) table wines)

——— COMBINE ———

A Parts of Wine (inclusive of	B Parts of Syrup flavouring)	Parts of Spirit Used				Resulting Alcohol Strength of Liqueur.
		68°	70°	80°	140°	
10	5	11	—	—	—	37°
10½	5	—	10½	—	—	37°
12	5	—	—	9	—	37°
16½	5	—	—	—	4½	38°
9½	5	11½	—	—	—	38°
10	5	—	11	—	—	38°
11½	5	—	—	9½	—	39°
9	5	12	—	—	—	39°
9½	5	—	11½	—	—	39°
11	5	—	—	10	—	40°
16	5	—	—	—	5	40°
8½	5	12½	—	—	—	40°
9	5	—	12	—	—	40°
7½	5	13½	—	—	—	41°
8	5	—	13	—	—	41°
10½	5	—	—	10½	—	41°
15½	5	—	—	—	5½	42°
7	5	14	—	—	—	42°
7½	5	—	13½	—	—	42°
10	5	—	—	11	—	42°
6½	5	14½	—	—	—	43°
7	5	—	14	—	—	43°
9½	5	—	—	11½	—	43°
15	5	—	—	—	6	44°
6	5	15	—	—	—	44°
6½	5	—	14½	—	—	44°
9	5	—	—	12	—	44°
5½	5	15½	—	—	—	45°
6	5	—	15	—	—	45°
8½	5	—	—	12½	—	45°
5	5	16	—	—	—	46°
5½	5	—	15½	—	—	46°
8	5	—	—	13	—	46°
14½	5	—	—	—	6½	47°
4½	5	16½	—	—	—	47°
5	5	—	16	—	—	47°
7½	5	—	—	13½	—	48°
4	5	17	—	—	—	48°
4½	5	—	16½	—	—	48°
7	5	—	—	14	—	49°
14	5	—	—	—	7	49°
3½	5	17½	—	—	—	49°
4	5	—	17	—	—	49°
6½	5	—	—	14½	—	50°

A Parts of Wine (inclusive of	B Parts of Syrup flavouring)	Parts of Spirit Used				Resulting Alcohol Strength of Liqueur.
		68°	70°	80°	140°	
3	5	18	—	—	—	50°
3½	5	—	17½	—	—	50°
6	5	—	—	15	—	51°
13½	5	—	—	—	7½	51°
2	5	19	—	—	—	51°
3	5	—	18	—	—	51°
5½	5	—	—	15½	—	52°
2½	5	—	18½	—	—	52°
1½	5	19½	—	—	—	52°
1	5	20	—	—	—	53°
2	5	—	19	—	—	53°
5	5	—	—	16	—	53°
13	5	—	—	—	8	54°
4½	5	—	—	16½	—	54°
½	5	20½	—	—	—	54°
1½	5	—	19½	—	—	54°
1	5	—	20	—	—	55°
4	5	—	—	17	—	56°
12½	5	—	—	—	8½	56°
½	5	—	20½	—	—	56°
3½	5	—	—	17½	—	57°
12	5	—	—	—	9	58°
3	5	—	—	18	—	58°
2½	5	—	—	18½	—	59°
11½	5	—	—	—	9½	60°
2	5	—	—	19	—	60°
1½	5	—	—	19½	—	61°
1	5	—	—	20	—	62°
11	5	—	—	—	10	63°
½	5	—	—	20½	—	63°
10½	5	—	—	—	10½	65°
10	5	—	—	—	11	67°
9½	5	—	—	—	11½	70°
9	5	—	—	—	12	72°
8½	5	—	—	—	12½	74°
8	5	—	—	—	13	76°
7½	5	—	—	—	13½	79°
7	5	—	—	—	14	81°
6½	5	—	—	—	14½	83°
6	5	—	—	—	15	86°
5½	5	—	—	—	15½	88°
5	5	—	—	—	16	90°
4½	5	—	—	—	16½	92°
4	5	—	—	—	17	95°
3½	5	—	—	—	17½	97°

ALCOHOL STRENGTH ADJUSTMENT TABLE "C"
(applicable to the use of 32° proof (or 18% alcohol by volume)
"base" wine)

―――――― COMBINE ――――――

A Parts of Wine (inclusive of flavouring)	B Parts of Syrup	68°	70°	80°	140°	Resulting Alcohol Strength of Liqueur.
13	5	8	—	—	—	37°
13½	5	—	7½	—	—	37°
15	5	—	—	6	—	37°
18	5	—	—	—	3	38°
12½	5	8½	—	—	—	38°
13	5	—	8	—	—	38°
14½	5	—	—	6½	—	38°
11½	5	9½	—	—	—	39°
12	5	—	9	—	—	39°
14	5	—	—	7	—	39°
17½	5	—	—	—	3½	40°
11	5	10	—	—	—	40°
11½	5	—	9½	—	—	40°
13½	5	—	—	7½	—	40°
10	5	11	—	—	—	41°
11	5	—	10	—	—	41°
13	5	—	—	8	—	41°
9½	5	11½	—	—	—	42°
10	5	—	11	—	—	42°
12½	5	—	—	8½	—	42°
17	5	—	—	—	4	42°
8½	5	12½	—	—	—	43°
9½	5	—	11½	—	—	43°
11½	5	—	—	9½	—	43°
8	5	13	—	—	—	44°
9	5	—	12	—	—	44°
11	5	—	—	10	—	44°
16½	5	—	—	—	4½	45°
7½	5	13½	—	—	—	45°
8	5	—	13	—	—	45°
10½	5	—	—	10½	—	45°
6½	5	14½	—	—	—	46°
7	5	—	14	—	—	46°
10	5	—	—	11	—	46°
16	5	—	—	—	5	47°
6	5	15	—	—	—	47°
6½	5	—	14½	—	—	47°
9½	5	—	—	11½	—	47°
5	5	16	—	—	—	48°
6	5	—	15	—	—	48°
9	5	—	—	12	—	48°
15½	5	—	—	—	5½	49°
4½	5	16½	—	—	—	49°
5	5	—	16	—	—	49°

A Parts of Wine (inclusive of flavouring)	B Parts of Syrup	Parts of Spirit Used				Resulting Alcohol Strength of Liqueur.
		68°	70°	80°	140°	
$8\frac{1}{2}$	5	—	—	$12\frac{1}{2}$	—	49°
$3\frac{1}{2}$	5	$17\frac{1}{2}$	—	—	—	50°
$4\frac{1}{2}$	5	—	$16\frac{1}{2}$	—	—	50°
8	5	—	—	13	—	50°
15	5	—	—	—	6	51°
3	5	18	—	—	—	51°
4	5	—	17	—	—	51°
$7\frac{1}{2}$	5	—	—	$13\frac{1}{2}$	—	51°
2	5	19	—	—	—	52°
3	5	—	18	—	—	52°
7	5	—	—	14	—	52°
$14\frac{1}{2}$	5	—	—	—	$6\frac{1}{2}$	53°
$1\frac{1}{2}$	5	$19\frac{1}{2}$	—	—	—	53°
$2\frac{1}{2}$	5	—	$18\frac{1}{2}$	—	—	53°
$6\frac{1}{2}$	5	—	—	$14\frac{1}{2}$	—	53°
1	5	20	—	—	—	54°
2	5	—	19	—	—	54°
6	5	—	—	15	—	54°
14	5	—	—	—	7	55°
1	5	—	20	—	—	55°
5	5	—	—	16	—	55°
$4\frac{1}{2}$	5	—	—	$16\frac{1}{2}$	—	56°
$13\frac{1}{2}$	5	—	—	—	$7\frac{1}{2}$	57°
4	5	—	—	17	—	57°
$3\frac{1}{2}$	5	—	—	$17\frac{1}{2}$	—	58°
13	5	—	—	—	8	59°
3	5	—	—	18	—	59°
$2\frac{1}{2}$	5	—	—	$18\frac{1}{2}$	—	60°
$12\frac{1}{2}$	5	—	—	—	$8\frac{1}{2}$	61°
2	5	—	—	19	—	61°
$1\frac{1}{2}$	5	—	—	$19\frac{1}{2}$	—	62°
12	5	—	—	—	9	63°
1	5	—	—	20	—	63°
$11\frac{1}{2}$	5	—	—	—	$9\frac{1}{2}$	65°
11	5	—	—	—	10	67°
$10\frac{1}{2}$	5	—	—	—	$10\frac{1}{2}$	69°
10	5	—	—	—	11	72°
$9\frac{1}{2}$	5	—	—	—	$11\frac{1}{2}$	74°
9	5	—	—	—	12	76°
$8\frac{1}{2}$	5	—	—	—	$12\frac{1}{2}$	78°
8	5	—	—	—	13	80°
$7\frac{1}{2}$	5	—	—	—	$13\frac{1}{2}$	82°
7	5	—	—	—	14	84°
$6\frac{1}{2}$	5	—	—	—	$14\frac{1}{2}$	86°
6	5	—	—	—	15	88°
$5\frac{1}{2}$	5	—	—	—	$15\frac{1}{2}$	90°

A Parts of Wine (inclusive of flavouring)	B Parts of Syrup	Parts of Spirit Used				Resulting Alcohol Strength of Liqueur.
		68°	70°	80°	140°	
5	5	—	—	—	16	92°
4½	5	—	—	—	16½	94°
4	5	—	—	—	17	96°
3½	5	—	—	—	17½	98°

ALCOHOL STRENGTH ADJUSTMENT TABLE "D"
(applicable to the use of 36° proof wines of the port type)

A Parts of Wine (inclusive of flavouring)	B Parts of Syrup	Parts of Spirit Used				Resulting Alcohol Strength of Liqueur.
		68°	70°	80°	140°	
14½	5	6½	—	—	—	37°
15	5	—	6	—	—	37°
16½	5	—	—	4½	—	37°
19	5	—	—	—	2	37°
14	5	7	—	—	—	38°
14½	5	—	6½	—	—	38°
16	5	—	—	5	—	38°
18½	5	—	—	—	2½	39°
13	5	8	—	—	—	39°
13½	5	—	7½	—	—	39°
15	5	—	—	6	—	39°
12½	5	8½	—	—	—	40°
13	5	—	8	—	—	40°
14½	5	—	—	6½	—	40°
18	5	—	—	—	3	41°
11½	5	9½	—	—	—	41°
12	5	—	9	—	—	41°
14	5	—	—	7	—	41°
10½	5	10½	—	—	—	42°
11½	5	—	9½	—	—	42°
13½	5	—	—	7½	—	42°
17½	5	—	—	—	3½	43°
10	5	11	—	—	—	43°
10½	5	—	10½	—	—	43°
13	5	—	—	8	—	43°
9	5	12	—	—	—	44°
9½	5	—	11½	—	—	44°
12	5	—	—	9	—	44°
17	5	—	—	—	4	45°
8	5	13	—	—	—	45°
9	5	—	12	—	—	45°
11½	5	—	—	9½	—	45°

A Parts of Wine (inclusive of	B Parts of Syrup flavouring)	Parts of Spirit Used				Resulting Alcohol Strength of Liqueur.
		68°	70°	80°	140°	
7½	5	13½	—	—	—	46°
8	5	—	13	—	—	46°
11	5	—	—	10	—	46°
16½	5	—	—	—	4½	47°
6½	5	14½	—	—	—	47°
7½	5	—	13½	—	—	47°
10½	5	—	—	10½	—	47°
6	5	15	—	—	—	48°
6½	5	—	14½	—	—	48°
10	5	—	—	11	—	48°
16	5	—	—	—	5	49°
5	5	16	—	—	—	49°
6	5	—	15	—	—	49°
9½	5	—	—	11½	—	49°
4	5	17	—	—	—	50°
5	5	—	16	—	—	50°
8½	5	—	—	12½	—	50°
15½	5	—	—	—	5½	51°
3½	5	17½	—	—	—	51°
4½	5	—	16½	—	—	51°
8	5	—	—	13	—	51°
2½	5	18½	—	—	—	52°
3½	5	—	17½	—	—	52°
7½	5	—	—	13½	—	52°
15	5	—	—	—	6	53°
1½	5	19½	—	—	—	53°
3	5	—	18	—	—	53°
7	5	—	—	14	—	53°
1	5	20	—	—	—	54°
2	5	—	19	—	—	54°
6½	5	—	—	14½	—	54°
14½	5	—	—	—	6½	55°
1½	5	—	19½	—	—	55°
5½	5	—	—	15½	—	55°
½	5	—	20½	—	—	56°
5	5	—	—	16	—	56°
14	5	—	—	—	7	57°
4½	5	—	—	16½	—	57°
4	5	—	—	17	—	58°
13½	5	—	—	—	7½	59°
3½	5	—	—	17½	—	59°
3	5	—	—	18	—	60°
13	5	—	—	—	8	61°
2	5	—	—	19	—	61°
1½	5	—	—	19½	—	62°

A Parts of Wine (inclusive of	B Parts of Syrup flavouring)	Parts of Spirit Used				Resulting Alcohol Strength of Liqueur.
		68°	70°	80°	140°	
12½	5	—	—	—	8½	63°
1	5	—	—	20	—	63°
½	5	—	—	20½	—	64°
12	5	—	—	—	9	65°
11½	5	—	—	—	9½	67°
11	5	—	—	—	10	69°
10½	5	—	—	—	10½	71°
10	5	—	—	—	11	73°
9½	5	—	—	—	11½	75°
9	5	—	—	—	12	77°
8½	5	—	—	—	12½	79°
8	5	—	—	—	13	81°
7½	5	—	—	—	13½	83°
7	5	—	—	—	14	85°
6½	5	—	—	—	14½	87°
6	5	—	—	—	15	89°
5½	5	—	—	—	15½	91°
5	5	—	—	—	16	93°
4½	5	—	—	—	16½	95°
4	5	—	—	—	17	97°

Chapter V

Getting the Flavour

EXCEPT for one thing, the term "liqueur" applies to potables which may be as varied, in respect of strength, colour and density, as any gathering of potential Miss Worlds facing Mecca. The notable exception is richness of flavour. This they must all possess: not just flavour with a small "f", but Flavour with a wallop. One that boosts whilst it bamboozles.

History in general has a rather tiresome habit of starting with the Chinese or the Chaldeans, but (although the Emperor Wu Ti *did* make a handsome contribution to a good many recipes by furthering the cultivation of coriander and certain other plants in moments slightly B.C.) liqueurs have, since long before the Chinese knew how to tell the time of their days, provided man's palate with something special to reflect upon. They made their advent so insidiously as to become one of the great pleasures of life without man himself being aware of their existence. In the drip of his cooking pot he tasted the rewards of the chase: the flavours of his quarry plus those of the grasses, leaves and wild plants upon which it had fed. He found the combination pleasant, good for his tummy and a push for his ego.

We ask no more of any liqueur to-day.

Though alcohol may serve, in certain cases, to strap concoctions together, and star-bright glints of colour look well in pony-sized goblets of hand-cut crystal, the soul of a liqueur is in its herbs. These, painstakingly searched for in, and gathered from, both likely and unlikely places all over the world, are the Public Relations Officers of the commercial liqueur producers. Enlisted in whole form so that they might be subject to close scrutiny before admission to the ranks, billeted in air-conditioned dormitories from which thermometers stick up like pokers, they are most carefully cosseted to ensure their fitness for any action to which they may be called. Those whose job it is to cater for erudite and discriminating palates know full well that all herb personalities depreciate rapidly with age and are often the sudden victims of heat, moisture, poor storage and a variety of pestilences that sap their essential oils, weaken their flavour and dim their fragrance.

One small measure of an inferior botanical (taken, perhaps, from a poor batch of European centaury or a dump load of cheap Chinese cassia) could quickly tumble a liqueur manufacturer's reputation built up over generations. Not for him, therefore, the "packaged specially for us" sticker which so often translates to "the better to nick you, dear customer". He knows what he wants and he speaks up and specifies.

The makers of nearly all the most famous liqueurs keep their recipes a secret. No one is permitted to learn, from them, the exact amount of aid and cheer that one herb gives to another in the vital formula. There are, however, no veils of secrecy to be torn apart in the telling of how their individual contributions are extracted and mingled for retention in the elixirs to which they are put.

Heading the list of Ways and Means is the process of distillation.

There are two types of still commercially employed: the traditional "Pot" still, basically unchanged over many centuries and continuing to be known by the alchemical term of "alembic" in certain parts, and the "Coffey" or patent-still invented around 1830 by an Irishman whose name it bears.

Liqueurs produced by distillation are also of two main types: those which are the outcome of one or more ingredients being assembled, mashed and fermented together to provide a wine which is subsequently vapourised and condensed, and those which are the result of a neutral spirit being re-distilled in the presence of flavourable and aromatic agents which impart their fragrances when infused or percolated by the hot liquor and/or its vapours.

On right:-

Pot-stills at Caol Ila Distillery, Isle of Islay, with view of the Isle of Jura across the sound. Caol Ila is one of over 40 distilleries which make malt whisky for blending companies in the DCL Group.

The following three photographs by courtesy of the Distillers Company Ltd.

Germinating Drum at Port Ellen Maltings. Showing part of the mechanism that causes the drums to rotate. The control panel (left) regulates the movement of the drum and the volume of conditioned air passed through it.

The Stillhouse at Caol Ila Distillery. The distillation of malt whisky is controlled by the stillman at the console in the foreground.

Typical of the former type are the liqueur brandies. These can be the distillate of apples, apricots, cherries, peaches, plums and, indeed, any fruit one cares to name. Cognac, based on the fermentation of juice gently pressed from especially acid grapes but taking the majority of its flavour from the oaks of the Limousin forest which supply the casks in which it matures, is brandy par excellence.

For the production of most reputable fruit brandies the old fashioned pot-stills are always used. Looking like huge copper turnips set on squat brick ovens, these insatiable brown babies take an average charge of two-hundred to two-hundred-and-fifty gallons of newly fermented wine: lees and all. A meander of pipes connects them to hooded condensers where flavours once grasped may be held. The ancient cornucopia-hatted cordial contriver would probably recognise them immediately, 'though his rheumy eyes might temporarily be perplexed at the sight of various supplementary lumps and bulges which have developed over the years. Of these, fairly standard is the chamber that surrounds the pipe carrying the hot vapours. Through this the cold, fermented liquor is obliged to circulate and be warmed prior to its general admission. Some distilleries go further in the provision of numerous bulbous excrescences on the vapour pipe just above the main body of the equipment. The extensive inner cooling surface of these separates the heavier fraction of the distillation (which drops back for further treatment) from the light fraction needing to be considerably reduced in temperature before it liquifies and which, therefore, passes on. In other cases the pot itself is divided into two separate compartments so that vapours leaving the lower chamber have no choice but to bubble through the liquid in the upper and partly recondense. When, however, sufficent heat has been transmitted to the liquid in the upper tank to prevent this phenomenon, the light fractions are able to escape up the vapour pipe towards the colling surfaces beyond.

An efficient cooling system is essential to liqueur distillations if some of the prized aroma is not to be squandered. In the case of cognac particularly, all distillations are carried out slowly at approximately 85°C. (185°F.). Since alcohol boils at a lower temperature than water, the alcohol vapours are the first to come away and are condensed back to liquid form on passing through cooled pipes. The heads and tails of the distillation are cut off and the resultant middle portion is run off with an alcohol content of 20% to 25%. This is returned to the pot and distilled for a second time, passing through exactly the same process as before and again being deprived of its head and tail. Only the real heart of the distillate remains: a liquid fire that will flay your mouth like a cat-o'-nine-tails should you be so unwise as to put it to the test. This is what the Nazis got when snooping around farmhouses of the French départments of the Charente and Charente Maritime, during the war years, demanding cognac.

In the case of apple brandy or Calvados (which the thirteenth-century chronicles of Charlemagne reported upon) the pot-still is charged with cider. The first throughput of this provides a main fraction of about 30% alcohol by volume, and a second distillation serves to just about double this strength. Somewhat brutal and belchful as it stands, the raw liquor demands a degree of dilution to take the curse off it: so an adjustment is made and, when slightly in excess of 50% alcohol, the spirit is run off into oaken barrels for a period of aging.

Applejack, the American equivalent of Calvados, has been produced in the United States since just about the time certain Pilgrim Fathers cocked a snook at The Old Folks At Home. The method of its production varies in no way from the manner described. Rumours to the effect that "congelation" (alcohol concentration by freezing: an idea first voiced by Paracelsus in the sixteenth century!) is commercially applied are completely false and are no more than the extension of an old legend.

The pot-stills of west-central Europe are kept busily employed in the distillation of Kirsch from a fermented mash of well-ripened morello cherries. In some formulations wild fruits, rather than those of a domestic nature, constitute the main bulk of the prepared must. In others, they are merely contributory agents to the general effect. Sometimes about one-third of the fruit stones are crushed and allowed to remain with the pulp during its fermentation period. This introduction provides an almond-tasting oil and (shades of Agatha Christie!) a small but innocuous amount of prussic acid: just sufficient to impart the required undertone. Alternatively, the distillate may receive the flavour boost of an almond essence.

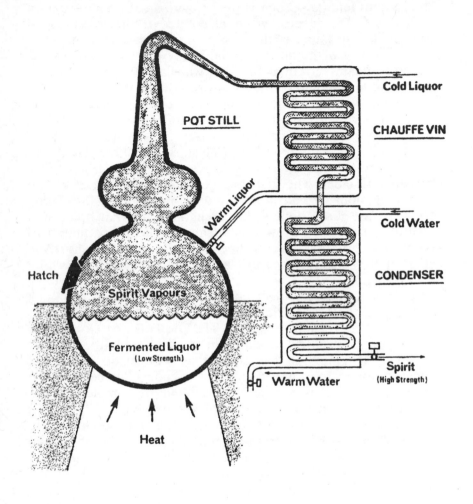

Diagram illustrating the general working principle of the Pot Still. The "Chauffe Vin" – employed for the warming of a wine prior to its entry to the main chamber – is a familiar addition to apparatus used for the production of cognac.

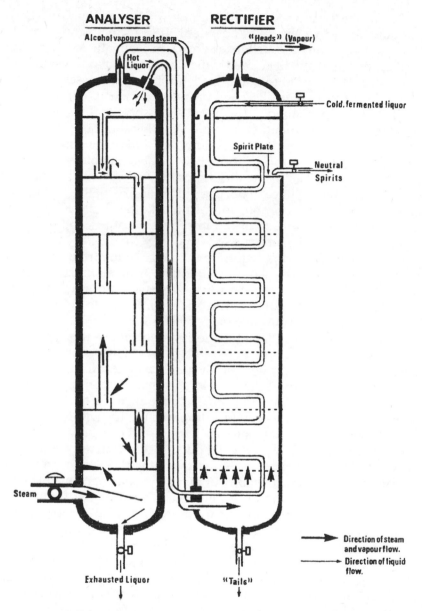

Diagram illustrating the general working principle of the Coffey Patent or Continuous Still.

According to the variety of fruit employed, the flavours of cherry liqueurs differ to a very marked extent. If, for example, the small, dark and sweet maraska cherries grown in Dalmatia are crushed, fermented and distilled in exactly the same manner as the morellos of Alsace, the resultant liqueur is identifiable as Maraschino. The final flavour of *any* distilled end product is, indeed, considerably influenced by even minor adjustments in respect of the nature and balance of the ingredients employed. Whether they be a part of the initial ferment, or be due for addition at some later stage, every single item listed in a formulation, be it ever so humble, will have a profound effect. The palate difference between Slivovitz (distilled from the fermented juice of pozega plums laced with the distinctive and bitter oil from a proportion of their kernels) and Klevovaca hangs on nought more than the introduction of a scoop or so of juniper berries at the time the still is initially charged.

In the case of liqueurs acquiring their distinction from processes of infusion and/or percolation rather than from an initial ferment of their basic constituents, the spirit used is almost invariably, but not necessarily, of a neutral nature: neutral, that is, to the extent of being free of any flavour save that of alcohol.

Many of the exotic "liqueurs monastique" are of this type and, since tradition dies hard, pot-stills are frequently employed for every stage of their production, a number of rectifications being required. In the case of the very largest manufactures, however, accountants rather than traditionalists are inclined to dictate the course events should take, and stills of the Coffey type have much to recommend them as regards efficiency and economy. They are conservative of heat whilst the old pot-still deals out its calories like gravy at a butcher's picnic. They provide the distiller with a much greater control over the quality of his end product, and enable him to recover more of the desirable constituents of the fermented liquor under treatment. Furthermore, they are capable of operating continuously and have a greatly increased output. So, in certain quarters at least, there is an increasing tendency to use stills of the Coffey type; at least for the development of the spirit itself, even though this may be switched, a few gallons at a time, to pots for re-distillation and final shaping in the presence of the botanicals assembled for it.

Grain alcohols, pot-stilled in ways that are frankly leisurely and distinctly fastidious, have gained their reputations on the strength of their originality. From district to district, as well as from country to country, marked differences of grain influence reveal themselves in the final analysis of customer participation. The mash of materials from which they are prepared may be conscientiously similar and the method of their processing correspondingly exact: nevertheless, local eccentricities crop out. Nobody really knows why.

A chemist will tell you that water distilled is like any other, and that alcohol from rye or maize or barley is not one jot different from alcohol distilled from other cereals. The traditionalist shakes his head and refuses to believe it. And most of the world's thinkers and drinkers are ranged on his side.

No wonder, then, that those who seek to retain a spirit's individual characteristics turn a blind eye to the economies that would follow the swapping of their inherited ancestral pots for some other type of still. On the other hand, it is not surprising that those seeking only alcohol in the nude see no trace of treachery in the use of an efficient device capable of dishing out a spirit virtually free from the intrusion of unrequired undertones.

Coffey stills consist of twin cylinders (known as the "analyser" and "rectifier" respectively) held together in a suitable framework. Each of these is divided into a number of chambers, one above the other. Steam admitted at the bottom of the analyser weaves its way, via opposingly situated vents, from one compartment to the next whilst fermented liquor, trickled in from the top, collects for a short time on the separating plates. Warmed by the rising steam and eventually reaching a depth that causes it to overflow down the vents, the wine splashes to the bottom of the lowest compartment. By this time all alcohol has been vapourised from it and has passed, with the steam, back to the top of the cylinder. The spent liquor, together with any steam that has condensed, flows away as waste.

The hot alcohol vapours and steam gathered at the highest level of the apparatus are now led by pipes from the analyser to the bottom of the rectifier. The plates which separate this into sections are dotted with perforations through which the hot vapours pass, bathing a pipe carrying the cold liquor on its way to processing. Condensation of the vapours is, thus, induced. The first to be affected are those comprising water and the high-boiling part of the

95

wine, principally composed of the inevitable but unrequired fusel-oil. Next, the main fraction liquefies on the pipes and drips to the plate immediately below. Lastly, at the top of the rectifier, the light fractions of the distillate condense or, if they are very light indeed, pass out to the atmosphere. So the operator may collect a fraction of any desired composition by the simple expedient of putting a catchment device in the right place at the opportune time.

All these shuntings, sidetrackings and switchings of Grade A to the main line so that it might ride 'till quality begins to taper, provide a spirit of high neutrality. If any unwanted influences do remain, these (known as "congenerics") are removed by filtration of the spirit through beds of charcoal.

The introduction of flavour and fragrance to alcohol strength usually takes place in a pot-still of modified design. This is first charged with the spirit due to be re-distilled within it and then the meticulously balanced medley of seeds, petals, leaves and other items of pervasive quality are admitted through hatches in its bulbous base or layered in trays fitted within the samovarish sweep of its copper top. Infused by the hot spirit or percolated by its vapours, their essential constituents are extracted from them and held for man's satisfaction at the last condensation stage.

Herbs such as allspice, aniseed, blessed thistle, calamus root, caraway, centaury, cinnamon, citronella, coriander, fennel, forget-me-not, gentian, ginger, horehound, juniper, lavender, mint, orange, rose, starwort, thyme and wormwood are well suited to infusion and percolation since they accept heat and suffer no harm when exposed to distillation temperatures. Others, however, are quickly degraded by it, suffering the loss of their essential oils with resultant flavour damage. There are, in consequence, occasions when distillation, infusion and percolation processes would be inappropriate. In such cases resort is made to the technique of maceration: one particularly suited to the needs of the amateur.

Maceration involves the preparation of ingredients, by crushing and soaking, exactly as for infusion except that, in this instance, the influence of heat is excluded. It is a process made much use of in the commercial manufacture of sweet and dry vermouths of all types, and has been the controlling factor of these companionable concoctions since 1786 when Antonio Benedetto Carpano of

Torino first began to cash in on their controlled production to meet the needs of King Victor Amadeus III, ruler of Piedmont.

When, in the late 1830's, the Piedmontese started exporting vermouth, its success was overwhelming and instantaneous. The French, bubbling and paddling, took to it like ducks. The South Americans expressed their affection for it so positively that to-day, in Argentina, the shank of each evening (the period between 6 p.m. and 9 p.m.) is called "the vermouth". The Manhattans and Martinis of the U.S.A. would never be the same without it, and in Britain a gin without an "It" or a "French" involved is considered almost as pointless as a "q" without a "u" to follow it.

From the point of view of the reader, vermouths are of particular interest since the established method of their production exactly relates, stage by stage, to routines which he may easily adopt for his own liqueur-making ends. Only the matter of final alcohol strength divides the vermouth-liqueur relationship and this, of course, is open to adjustment in accordance with the Alcohol Strength Adjustment Tables of previous chapters or to whatever extent may be considered appropriate.

The base wine employed, running around 23°–25° proof, is usually white and of insignificant flavour. Fruit vermouths, chiefly of Dutch or German manufacture, demand by implication a substantial grounding on fruit wines fermented from grape juice and mixed fruit compounds. These, however, are exceptions to the general rule. Though some sweet vermouths of the Italian type are made from white muscatel wines which have been fermented for a restricted period only so that, whilst supplying only a small amount of alcohol, they have a high proportion of their natural grape sugars to offer, most have their origins in the same white wine as those from which the dry "French" versions stem, and achieve their colour and sweetness from additions of caramel or cochineal and surgar-syrup. Of this latter agent, the sweet vermouths receive a dose four or five times more generous than their drier counterparts, and even these, in their final palate assessment, are far from being as dry as the term implies when associated with an ordinary wine of table type.

Citric acid (used according to circumstances but frequently employed at a rate equivalent to a half-saltspoonful per 26 fluid ounce bottle) is also added to prevent the end product tasting flabby and somewhat medicinal.

According to where you look you can locate vermouths as self-effacing as 26° proof or as pushful as 35°. Most of them come out somewhere in between (28°–32°) under the influence of booster doses of neutral spirits. As regards the herbs themselves, one to four ounces per gallon (assembled from substances as diverse as allspice, blessed thistle, calamus root, centaury, cinchona, cinnamon, coriander, elder flowers, forget-me-not, gentian, horehound, starwort, wormwood and a passel of others) are put to service according to the composite effect aimed for. If, for example, a more bitter result is the objective, the wormwood ration is upped and the amount of cinnamon and coriander compensatingly reduced. Peerless appetite whetters, on the other hand, call for quinine additions or circumspect allowances of peruvian bark. Whatever the combination might be, the transference of flavour from solids to solution is brought about by the maceration process. Some producers infuse the herbs into the neutral spirit. The result is an extract available for use as required and usually so pungent and potent that a sample drop or two will curl your tongue and leave its effect with you for the rest of the day. Others prepare the fortified wine first, then soak the herbs in this for several months.

Packeted herbs, ready-balanced in accordance with brand recipes aimed at providing flavours closely approaching those of certain well-known commercial products, are available for amateur use. These, securely contained in a small piece of scalded muslin or other suitable material, are merely suspended in a jar of wine (appropriately sweetened to meet personal taste and/or the nature – vermouth or liqueur – of the product aimed at) for whatever period of time is necessary to allow for the transference, by maceration, of their volatile and aromatic constituents. Personal decision, guided by day-to-day sippings, must here play its part. It is, however, necessary to allow for the flavour reduction that will be occasioned by whatever quantity of neutral spirit is finally added.

In the case of vermouths (particularly those resulting from the use of the Liqueur Wine-base receipe previously detailed) no further fortification may be considered necessary. Whatever wine is used, two fluid ounces of vodka (or one fluid ounce of Polish spirit) per twenty-six fluid ounce bottle will prove adequate. This, however, is a casual approach and, particularly in the matter of liqueur production, one is well advised to be more precise. Though the average amateur seeks mathematic exercise like Custer needed Indians, results of consistent effect can only follow the development of expertise and it is worthwhile to remain in full awareness of the alcohol strengths involved at every stage of the process.

We start, then, by sweetening a measured quantity of wine to taste, noting (a) its volume *prior* to sugar addition, and (b) its volume *after* sugar addition. Providing we are aware of the alcohol strength of the wine used and on the basis of these two measurements we can assess the resultant strength of the composed syrup by putting to use the following formula:

$$\frac{A \times B}{C}$$

where A = No. of ounces of wine, B = Alcohol strength of wine, and C = No. of ounces of syrup.

For example: supposing we have taken 20 fl. oz. of a 21° proof commercial wine and have dissolved in it 8 oz. of sugar to produce a syrup of 30 fl. oz. volume, then:

$$\frac{20 \times 21}{30} = \frac{420}{30} = 14 \text{ or, in our terms, } 14° \text{ proof.}$$

The herbs are now allowed to macerate in the sweetened wine until the desired amount of flavour has been extracted from them, at which time all that remains for the completion of the object is the incorporation of a fortifying spirit.

The amount of this needing to be used will depend upon (a) the nature of the neutral spirit employed (vodka or Polish spirit), and (b) the ultimate strength aimed for in the completed product. As regards the latter consideration, we may obtain fair guidance by referring to Alcohol Strength Adjustment Table B. Scanning the "resultant Strength" column of this we find, for example, that a final product of 63° proof may be obtained by combining 10 fl. oz. of Polish spirit with 16 fl. oz. of a sweetened and flavoured wine

99

(the combined total of parts suggested by columns A and B). In accordance with this balance, therefore, let us be disposed to measure off 16 fl. oz. of our 14° proof wine-and-sugar syrup and to it add 10 fl. oz. of 140° proof Polish spirit, checking the exact result of is composition by means of a further simple mathematical formula:

$$\frac{(E \times D) + (F \times G)}{E + F}$$

where E = No. of ounces of wine/sugar syrup, D = Alcohol strength of wine/sugar syrup, F = No. of ounces of spirit, and G = Alcohol strength of spirit.

In this imagined instance, the sum would be as follows:

$$\frac{(16 \times 14) + (10 \times 140)}{16 + 10} = \frac{1624}{26} = 62.5° \text{ proof.}$$

The result in this case is remarkably close (within half a degree, in fact!) of the Table B forecast. Even had we used 12 oz. of sugar to secure the syrup sweetness desired, the final strength of the liqueur would have been less than two degrees away from the Table's assessment, and in no case will the result be excessively adrift. Those readers not insistent upon precise final strengths calculated in terms of decimals may, therefore, feel inclined to dispose of all calculations, accepting the Table B provided as their sole guide and mentor.

Amongst the several reliable brands of packeted herbs available for the flavouring of amateur vermouths are those supplied under name of "Winemaster" (manufactured by Ritchie Products of Rollestone Rd., Burton-on-Trent, DE13 0JX) covering the production of both Italian and French types, and "Semplex" (Semplex Home Brews Ltd., Old Hall Works, Stuart Road, Higher Tranmere, Birkenhead) which offers Italian vermouth powders of specific types: Torino Extra, Torino Export, Concorrenza and Bianco.

Herbs suited to the needs of Green Chartreuse and Yellow Chartreuse-type liqueurs are marketed under the "Winemaster" label, whilst "Vinaide" powdered herbs of Chartreuse and Benedictine-type composition are the product of Vinaide Brewing & Food Products of 31 Blackfriars Rd., Salford, M3 5JQ.

Chapter VI

Enzymes, Esters and Essences

STRAWBERRIES, raspberries, red currants, gooseberries and the dark-skinned fruits such as blackcurrants, blackberries and black cherries are typical of basic ingredients capable of achieving a special quality when worked upon by processes devoid of heat application. Our Great-Grandmamas shuffled many of them, fork-pricked and bleeding, into stone jars, sandwiched them between layers of sugar or powdered sugar-candy, and left them to slowly disintegrate under the influence of neat spirits. Nature and infinite patience provided the result: indefinite quantities of syrupy fruit gins and brandies of indeterminate strength. As for expecting any two batches to turn out alike, that would have been as unreasonable as asking Lady Luck to be regular.

There are still those who follow the old ways of hit-or-miss, particularly so far as the manufacture of cherry brandy is concerned. It should, however, always be borne in mind that whilst liqueurs of excessive sweetness and inadequate strength are all very well if one likes such concoctions, they should be produced by intent; never by accident. The difference between being amateur and amateurish is considerable and rests, mainly, on the application of a little accountancy to the balancing of basic ingredients, one against the other, when the time comes for their being put together. There are, also, two elementary rules worthy of note and applicable to liqueur manufacture of any kind:

1. It is common sense, in following any recipe, to put the less costly ingredients together first. Then, if you make a mistake, the offending material can be thrown away before expensive spirits have converted an accident into a financial loss or, even worse, a social catastrophe.

2. All other considerations apart and purely for the sake of the chemistry, always add the spirits last when assembling any

combination of which fruit juices and/or sweetening matter are ingredients.

In the construction of a fruit liqueur such as a cherry brandy or sloe gin we should focus our initial attention not so much on the solid weight of fruit available as on the volume of fully-flavoured juice we are capable of persuading from it. The subsequent stages of juice-to-syrup conversion and eventual fortification can then follow in accordance with the rules for action we have adopted.

Fruits lightly pulped and treated with suitable enzyme additives quickly break down to a smooth purée from which their juice may easily be pressed and racked off for storage or immediate filtration. A remarkably small amount of material goes to waste and the average yield is not only of better colour and clarity than would be a juice expressed by heat application or mechanical means, but also has a richer flavour. Further, it flows at least twenty-five per cent more generously than it would under any other form of treatment: a matter, of considerable importance to the commercial manufacturer who seeks to make four tons of fruit supply the benefit of five.

The enzymes, used for the bringing about of this very satisfactory state of affairs are pectinases (obtainable under such brand names as Pektolase and Pectinol) employed in conjunction with one lumbered as Pectinglycosidase but fortunately available to the amateur under the less tongue-twisting title of "Rohament P".

Enzymes mostly take their names from the substances they act upon with the suffix "-ase". In accordance with this simple but effective scheme of identification, pectinases control a group of closely related substances known as the Pectins. These (methylated-polygalacturonic acids if you must know) are remarkably commonplace, being present in some vegetables and all fruits, their quantity varying according to the nature of the fruit itself. Bananas, for instance, are insignificantly provided. Strawberries, on the other hand, contain slightly more, whilst apples, apricots and plums of every variety contain them in considerable quantity.

Under normal circumstances their presence goes unremarked. A simple test, however, quickly reveals their existence.

To one tablespoonful of fruit juice add half-a-tablespoonful of sugar and three-quarters of a teaspoonful of Epsom Salts. Stir the mixture until all the salts and sugar are dissolved: then leave it undisturbed for five minutes. If, within this time, the syrup sets to a jellylike mass, the presence of pectin in considerable quantity is evidenced. If the resultant mass is soft to the touch, then the amount of pectin is fairly average. Should no setting at all result, pectin influence is comparatively small but still warrants a degree of control if we are to utilise the parent fruit to our maximum benefit.

During the day-to-day conditions of a fruit's growth and development, Nature itself provides the restraint of inbuilt enzymic supervision. When, however, this sentinel agency suffers extinction (as it does through the application of excessive heat: when fruit is scalded by means of boiling water, for example, or during the course of its being converted to jam) the pectins are released and reveal their ability to create a state of jell in high concentrations of sugar and acid. This circumstance, though made much use of by the housewife in her provision of conserves for the family table, is directly opposed to the requirements of the wine and liqueur maker who seeks only the maximum flavour transference of a generously flowing juice unmarred by hazes which no amount of fussing and finicking with filters or finings will clear.

In the quality-control laboratories of commercial manufacturies, the progressive effect of enzyme influence on the pectin content of juices under treatment is constantly studied, either by viscosity measurement (involving the use of an instrument not unreasonably called a viscosimeter) or by the deliberate inducement of pectin precipitation.

At suitable intervals after the enzyme has been added, samples are drawn and vigorously shaken with three to four times their volume of methylated spirits (92% alcohol) or an equal amount of industrial spirits (95% alcohol). In the case of certain fruits (blackcurrants, for example) only half these additions may sometimes be sufficient to bring about an immediate effect indicating pectin presence: the development of off-white strings and clots which, in extreme cases, coagulate to a solid mass within a matter of minutes. If no such precipitation or cloudiness occurs, this absence of reaction is taken to indicate a complete decomposition of the sample's pectin content. Even so (because minor traces may take some time to reveal themselves) no test is regarded as negative 'till an hour or so has elapsed.

According to how they are employed, anti-pectin enzymes offer a choice of service. Dependent upon the result desired a partial or complete decomposition of pectin may be achieved. In the case of liqueur production, nothing less than the complete removal of all pectin influence is acceptable. Flavoured and aromatised solutions scheduled to meet substantial quantities of alcohol en route to the bottle must be capable of facing up to the introduction without gelatinizing or otherwise falling apart.

Since many fruits contain varying amounts of pectin depending upon the nature of the soil from which they came and their degree of ripeness at the time of being harvested, the large-scale commercial manufacturer, scheduling for bulk loads of a thousand kilos or more at a pressing, needs to keep a wary eye on a number of factors which influence the quantity of enzyme used, the temperature at which it is put to action, and the time taken for a satisfactory result to be obtained. The amateur, working with only a few pounds of fruit, may confidently follow the printed instructions supplied along with the pectinase enzyme of his choice, the dosage rate and working temperature advised being sufficiently average to cope with the majority of situations. There are, however, certain general observations to be made:

Most brands of anti-pectin enzyme are available in both liquid and dry powder form, the latter being based on either diatomaceous earth or glucose.

The liquid type, since it may be added directly to, and is easily involved throughout, the fruit mass under treatment, is the most convenient to use. It does, however, suffer the disadvantage of needing to be stored in a refrigerator (0° Centigrade) if a shelf life of twelve months is expected of it. Powdered enzymes, on the other hand, merely need to be kept away from direct sunlight (preferably in dark glass or corrugated-paper wrapped jars fitted with screw-caps) when they will maintain their quality for a similar period in ambient temperatures not exceeding 15° Centigrade (59° Fahrenheit).

Glucose-based powders offer an obvious advantage in being completely soluble but are less satisfactory than the earth-bound type in dealing with soft fruits. These, difficult to handle during pressing because they break down to a slippery consistency, need to have their substance made more responsive to a squeezing process. The quantity of slightly abrasive material provided by the diatomaceous-based enzyme supplies the necessary aid. In the event of liquid or glucose-type anti-pectins being the only kinds available, diatomaceous silica (sold by some stockists as "kieselguhr" and by others, wishing to maintain a stiff upper lip, as "wine filtering powder") can, of course, be separately added and will be found to make a worthwhile contribution.

Enzymes are active in the usual acidity of fruits, even when this is subject to reasonable dilution as, for example, in the case of dried apricots or figs which need to be soaked and/or heated in a small amount of water prior to being crushed. They also operate successfully at all temperatures between 20° Centigrade (68° Fahrenheit) and 50° Centigrade (122° Fahrenheit), accomplishing their effect more rapidly as temperature increases but, at the same time, giving flow to a juice of darker colour.

Because all fruits contain more or less pectin according to their degree of ripeness when picked, it is impossible to lay down any hard and fast rule as to how long they should be processed. The only spot-on answer to this question lies in the alcohol-pectin test described. The following Table may, however, be accepted as a very general guide based on a short range of the most commonly employed soft fruits harvested at the moment of their optimum condition.

Providing one has the necessary means of weighing out materials in precise metric quantities (and there are a number of inexpensive but accurate scales available, one such being the Dr. Oetker 777 Mini-Balance) the average enzyme addition of two-and-a-half grams per six pounds of fruit may, of course, be proportionately reduced in accordance with whatever lesser quantity of material is due for treatment. This insignificant economy is not, however, advised. In dealing with enzymes, generosity pays off to one's advantage and, indeed, the addition suggested may safely be doubled if the fruit to be worked upon is known to have an exceptionally high pectin content or has been picked when under or over-ripe.

FRUIT	Average amount of Enzyme added per 6 lb. of Fruit	Temperature (°Centigrade)	Temperature (°Fahrenheit)	Time: (hours)
Blackcurrant	2.5 grams (half teaspoonful)	20	68	2–8
Blackcurrant	,,	50	122	2–6
Redcurrant	,,	20	68	2–8
Redcurrant	2.5 grams	45	113	1–2
Gooseberry	,,	20	68	2–8
Gooseberry	,,	50 •	122	1–4
Strawberry	,,	20	68	1–2
Strawberry	,,	45	113	1
Blackberry	,,	20	68	6–12
Blackberry	,,	45	113	1–3
Raspberry	,,	20	68	3–6
Raspberry	,,	45	113	1–2
Cherry	,,	20	68	3–6
Cherry	,,	45	113	1–2

Whatever quantity of enzyme is used, this is best incorporated when dissolved or suspended in a small amount of free juice or water prior to its addition to the main bulk of materials. These may, at the same time, be sulphited (at the rate of one Campden Tablet for every four to six pounds weight) for their protection against the possibility of bacterial contamination. An initial tendency for some fruits to be slightly bleached by the sulphite is no cause for concern since their full colour will return within a very short while.

Frequent stirring of the combined mass during its treatment is essential if substantial temperature differences within it, leading to uneven processing, are to be avoided.

So much for the anti-pectins. Now for the Rohament P . . .

In days long gone, when country folk were a-bed by sundown but out and about to meet the early morning mists, there was a pretty tradition to the effect (expressed by some anonymous poet caught in something between a literary whoop and a hiccough of ectasy) that only fruit picked at sunrise had the "tang of a maiden's first kiss and some of its shyness". More prosaically, it was generally supposed to contain a spit more juice.

Rohament "P" is the enzyme used to speed the reduction of fruit to a purée state and is applied at a dosage rate of half-a-teaspoonful per six pounds weight of material. In this case fresh strawberries are under experimental treatment, being quickly reduced to a mess of individual cells from which their juice is easily pressed but which retains all the vitamins, natural sugars, colour and flavour of its source.

To-day, those whose job it is to wring the orchards and hedgerows for what they might contain leave tradition to the burks, suppose less, and pin their faith to an enzyme, Rohament P, that falls into an effective collaboration with any type or brand of anti-pectin with which it may be partnered. This breaks down and dissolves the cellular connective tissues that provide our fruits and vegetables with their familiar shape and form. In the possession of this ability it is closely linked with a number of other enzyme substances which, long before they were identified and named, smoothed the path of man in a variety of similar ways.

The sweetness of the date, for example, is entirely due to the presence, within the fruit, of Cytase: an enzyme which reduces the reserve cellulose of the germinating seed to easily digestible sugars. Papain, a further close relative found in the milky latex of the papaya plant, has long served generations of Caribbean folk in their domestic chores following the discovery that the toughest meat might be rendered tender by being wrapped in the leaves of the plant or rubbed with its juice.

The action of Rohament P upon the cellular tissues of fruit and vegetables is not dissimilar. Applied at a dosage rate of half-a-teaspoonful per six pounds weight of material (and if your hand shakes over-generously whilst dispensing the ration it doesn't matter!) it immediately works to break down the structure of the mass, reducing this to a purée state of individual cells obliged to relinquish their fluid content which, clarified by simultaneous pectinase activity, flows freely as a juice retaining all the vitamins, natural sugars, colour and flavour of its source.

Rohament P unreservedly accepts the same environmental conditions as the enzyme with which it is teamed, providing maximum juice release if put to work at the lower temperatures listed in the anti-pectin Table and left for a period at least as long as that considered appropriate for complete pectin elimination. Used at the higher temperatures mentioned, full colour release may be attained after only one or two hours but, in the interests of flavour extraction, the times quoted against these can well afford to be exceeded without fear of matters going awry, extended processing merely having the effect of thinning the juice and rendering it more amenable to separation from desiccated waste matter when the slop of ravished material and moisture is hand-pressed through a previously scalded linen cloth (corners brought together in tramps'-breakfast style) or jelly-bag. In any event, straining and filtration of the juice (if employed in preference to its being allowed to stand for a while 'till all small particles of pulp have settled as a deposit) is best conducted as hot as possible within the range of 66°–72° Centigrade (151°–162° Fahrenheit). These temperatures, though high enough to speed the process and inactivate the enzymes themselves, will not impair the colour, flavour or vitamin content of juice subjected (for a short, sharp moment only) to their influence.

The processes detailed take longer in the telling than in their application. Most of the fruit brandies and gins formerly produced by old-style country methods lend themselves very simply to a contemporary three-stage construction plan. By way of example, let us compare the alternative ways of making Cherry Brandy:

Making Cherry Brandy in the traditional way. Alternate layers of pricked Morello Cherries and Sugar (or well-powdered sugar-candy) at the rate of 6 oz. per pound of fruit are funnelled into a suitable jar prior to being soaked with brandy and left to mature for at least four months under seal. One or two cloves and sometimes a trace of citric acid are optional extras.

A traditional recipe, reproduced verbatim from a household encyclopedia of unspecified date, reads as follows:-

Ingredients   Morello Cherries, Sugar or Sugar-candy, Brandy.

Method   Remove the stalks from the cherries, which should be ripe and sound, prick them with a large needle or fork, and drop them into a bottle. To every pound of fruit allow 6 oz. of sugar or well-powdered sugar-candy. Put this in and fill up the bottle with brandy. The bottle should be three parts full of cherries.

Cork down and keep for at least four months, shaking the bottle every now and again.

Since the amount of flavour transferred to the brandy is entirely dependent upon an unknown quantity of juice and the extractive abilities of a vaguely specified volume of spirit, it is not to be wondered at that authors of such formulations decline to attribute any specific strength to the end product of their recommendations. In the application of contemporary processes, however, the matter of final strength is the first consideration, selected by reference to the Alcohol Strength Adjustment Table "A" provided on pages 53 and 54 of Chapter III.

Supposing that 35° proof be accepted as adequately companionable, 10½ fl. oz. of pure Morello Cherry juice will be required in accordance with the forecast of Column A. So,

1. By means of a heavy kitchen fork or the back of a wooden spoon, lightly crush one pound of fruit in a graduated measure to produce a rough slop approximately 18 fl. oz. volume. Pour off a little of the free juice and in this dissolve one Campden Tablet prior to adding half-a-teaspoon each of Rohament P and some anti-pectin enzyme. Stir well and add to the contents of the measure, stirring rapidly during its introduction to ensure its even dispersion throughout the mass. Cover the measure with a clean cloth and place in a warm atmosphere.

2. After 24-hours, transfer the resulting purée to a saucepan and bring to a simmering temperature of 66°–72° Centigrade (151°–162° Fahrenheit) to inactivate its enzyme content. Then, whilst it is still hot, place the purée in a scalded jelly-bag. Clear juice (directed into a measure) will immediately start to flow freely, but hand pressure should be applied as soon as the cooling mass permits.

When 10½ fl. oz. of juice have been measured off, add 4 oz. of sugar and stir to dissolve. The resulting volume of syrup should now read 13 fl. oz. in accordance with Column B of the Strength Adjustment Table, but in the event of any variation, a suitable adjustment can be made from whatever juice is available.

3. When the syrup is quite cold, add 13 fl. oz. of brandy as directed in Column D of the Table.

The result of these three-stage manoeuvres will be a liqueur open to the acceptance of immediate engagements. That is not to say it won't improve immeasurably under storage conditions. Each week of passing time works wonders as regards the involvement of one ingredient with another. Personal decision must, however, answer the question of whether a virtually "instant" product should be put away behind glass for a reasonable period, or be made use of at once. After the enthusiast has sipped enough samples to form his own judgements, he may decide that this or that item is best served from a bucket and dipper, drunk from the bottle, or taken by injection. These are matters of personal taste, and a book of this nature can only serve as a general guide to the various ways and means of indulging its readers' own preferences.

Regarding the final palate effect of a Cherry Brandy, for instance: some like this to be finely laced with an undertone of cloves, and one or two of these may be introduced to the purée at the time of its being brought to simmering point prior to pressing.

The prussic acid influence of cracked cherry kernels may be simulated by the addition of one or two drops of almond essence to the product. The brandy employed may itself be prepared, some days in advance of its requirement, by being used to soak the petal-thin peel-shavings (no white pith) of one or two oranges. These, macerated in the spirit 'till translucent, will donate the distinctive piquancy of their oil content. In the case of experimental formulations found to be out of balance in respect of their flavour/alcohol relationship (and in no concoction should spirit be allowed to dominate the situation) Cherry Brandy extracts, redolent of fruit harvested at the peak of its perfection, are available for boosting purposes and may, indeed, be put to service as the principal flavouring constituent employed.

The production of liqueurs and vermouths by the process of cold-compounding is self-explanatory, merely involving the addition of essential oils, balanced herb mixtures or concentrates to spirits or wine-and-spirit solutions which are then filtered, sweetened and coloured as necessary. It has the twin virtues of simplicity and adaptability. Conducted in accordance with the precepts of Tables B, C, and D (pages 78–84) it provides the veriest newcomer to home liqueur-making with a means of closely matching some of the most famous boons to the palate of man known to our world.

The concentrates available for both large-scale commercial and amateur use divide into two groups: those that are truly the extract of vegetable materials (such as herbs, aromatic plants, flowers, seeds, fruit kernels and the selected fruits themselves), and those based on flavours which, though authentic, have laboratory origins. In both cases the agents of their effect (occurring naturally in the one and scientifically produced to meet the needs of the other) are the alcohols carbonyls, acetals, esters and other volatile substances involved.

Research into the chemical content of plant life is continually going forward, accumulating en route a deal of information put to use by those whose job it is to duplicate, in test-tubes, the best of nature's smells and essences. These men of dedicated talent possess the skills if not the loftier inspirations of great painters, putting their noses to a scent and identifying its component parts as a Cézanne or Constable might assess the shadow of a passing cloud in terms of primary colour. The poets amongst us might invest with romance a warm June evening heavy with the breath of red roses. Breath of red roses nothing! The perfumery chemist will recognise it as the complex whiff of geraniol, citronellol, citral, eugenol, linalol, nerol, and various alcohols and aldehydes!

A garden-grown strawberry, brought to succulence by natural means and cloche-protected from a too-close acquaintance with the cat next door, is dependent for its flavour upon no less than one-hundred-and-thirty-nine volatile constituents bearing names such as cyclohexane, phenylethanol and dimethyoxymethane together with hyphenated constructions ("trans-3-Hexan-1-yl n-hexanoate" for example) of even greater complication. Many of its component influences are also present in other fruits. Benzyl acetate, a jasmine-like ester, is contained in Oil of Neroli (embracing a number of extracts derived from orange flowers), Cassie, and the first distillation of essential oil from Cananga-

112

odorata flowers. Benzaldehyde, one of the strawberry's carbonyls, is also the chief constituent of peach, apricot and bitter-almond kernels.

Capsaicin is the active bitter principle of a soluble essence obtained from Capsicums (the chillies of pods of a weed indigenous to India but cultivated in most tropical countries) and allied red peppers. Carvone, frequently used in the flavouring of liqueurs and cordials, occurs in spearmint and dill oils. Cinnamic aldehyde, occurs naturally in Cinnamon and Cassia Bark. Another aldehyde, citral, is present (to the extent of 70–85%) in the distilled oil of Verbena which also contains geraniol, citronellal, methyl-heptenone and limonene.

Citronellol, an alcohol, occurs naturally in geranium as well as rose petals. The roots of Dandelion plants are rich in taraxcin and inulin. Decylic aldehyde is contained in the expressed oils of sweet oranges, and eugenol is the chief constituent of cloves.

These facts are noted, partly as a matter of interest but, to a greater extent, in defence of the synthetics. The reasoning is this: if the fruit we seek to dredge with sugar and drown in cream is reliant upon ethyl acetate for the richness of its flavour, the same ester, used as a basis for the production of an artificial raspberry essence, should be no cause for concern.

The close relationship of the chemically contrived esters, aldehydes and acetals to those which develop naturally, during the maturing of a wine for example, may be further underlined by a comparison of the processes involved. In both cases the fragrant, pleasantly aromatic and volatile substances are the result of a marriage between major and minor constituents, oxidation being the consummating influence.

A new wine, set aside under circumstances that allow a small amount of air to be present, acquires its quality and bouquet owing to the fact that a trace of its ethyl alcohol content is oxidised to (a) acetaldehyde, and (b) acetic acid. Concurrently, the minor amount of its other higher alcohols, or a small part of them, are worked upon to produce *their* respective aldehydes and acids. During the course of the celebratory whoop-up that follows, when all members of the family meet together for the social binge that all marriages are inclined to induce, the acetaldehyde fraction seeks a partner from amongst its cousin aldehydes and, under the influence of

113

alcohol, kicks over the traces to produce a host of little acetals and esters.

The commercially applied esterification process is merely a deliberate stage-management of this.

Based on the knowledge that alcohols combine with acids to form new substances corresponding to the salts of inorganic chemistry, an alcohol and an acid are heated together in the presence of a dehydrating agent, the mixture then being fractionally distilled to produce the ester required. Thus: Ethyl Alcohol + Acetic Acid = Ethyl Acetate. If, on the other hand, Amyl Alcohol and Acetic Acid are treated in the same way, the result of their union is Amyl Acetate: known as Banana Oil (or sometimes Pear Oil) and much used in the preparation of pear and cherryade essences. Other flavouring principles, met with more frequently during the course of a day's palate experience than might be supposed, are:

Amyl Butyrate   sometimes labelled as Apricot Oil,

Amyl Caprionate   frequently used in the preparation of simulated cognacs,

Amyl Heptylate   an ester of very pronounced "fruity" bouquet appropriate to the manufacture of many essences,

Amyl Isovalerate   redolent of apples and generally referred to as Apple Oil,

Amyl Salicylate   an ester with a clover bouquet,

Anis Aldehyde   conveying the scent of hawthorn blossoms,

Benzyl Acetate   one of the natural strawberry constituents but, on its own, of jasmine-like influence,

Benzyl Butyrate   sometimes used in banana, peach and apricot formulations,

Benzyl Formate   an ester of cinnamon flavour,

Benzyl Proprionate   an alternative simulation of banana flavour,

Benzyl Valerianate   an ester with a rose-like bouquet,

Citronellyl Acetate   conveying the pervasive quality of freshly-gathered lavender,

Citronellyl Formate   sometimes used to supplement preparations based on the scents of rose and bergamot,

Citronellyl Propionate   similar in its application to the above,

Duodecylic Aldehyde   frequently blended with orange essences to greatly increase the quality of bouquet,

Ethyl Benzoate   an ester used in meadosweet essences and a useful fixative in perfumery.

Ethyl Butyrate   the principal constituent of artificial pineapple,

Ethyl Cinnamate   the primary source of apricot bouquets,

Ethyl Formate   an ester with a rum flavour, prepared by the distillation of alcohol, glycerin and oxalic acid,

Ethyl Salicylate   providing a wintergreen bouquet of delicate character,

Ethyl Sebacate   an ester used as a fruit bouquet,

Ethyl Valerianate   employed in fruit beverages demanding a pineapple influence,

Geranyl Acetate   another of the esters providing a lavender bouquet,

Geranyl Butyrate   an ester of marked rose bouquet,

Geranyl Formate   identifiable as the source of wild-rose bouquet,

Geranyl Proprionate   another influence behind the scent of bergamot,

Heliotropin   an aldehyde providing the aroma of heliotrope and sometimes blended with vanilla flavours,

Linalyl Acetate   closely resembles natural bergamot in which it is contained,

Methyl Anthranilate   the methyl ester of anthranilic acid, occurring naturally in neroli and jasmine and used in the artificial types of these oils. In great dilution it resembles the flavour of muscat grapes and is used in a wide range of grape flavours, being also employed to fortify natural grape beverages,

Methyl Salicylate   occurs naturally in wintergreen and is obtained synthetically by distilling methyl alcohol, salicylic acid and sulphuric acid. Employed in sarsaparilla and birch-beer type beverages,

Nonylic Alcohol   has a rose bouquet and is sometimes blended with orange and neroli extracts,

Octylic Alcohol   of markedly lemon-like bouquet,

Phenyl-Propyl Butyrate   Has a jasmine odour and is sometimes used in beverages to provide bouquet.

The effect of a label depends less on colour and artistic ability than ingenuity and general neatness.
In the case of all bottles illustrated above, Letraset was used.

Chapter VII

For Instant Enjoyment

THE time has come to step out a bit, and those anxious to head for Gracious Living in a determined way can do no better than start by making immediate use of the wide range of carefully contrived flavouring extracts and essences available to them.

Some, it has been said, are entirely based on materials of a vegetable nature. Others, fractionally cheaper, are the result of scientific probings and assimilation. All will prove true to the promise of their label and the name of the liqueur upon it.

Here, then, are seventy-nine elixirs for your eloquence, coded according to their source of supply:

TYPE	LIQUEUR	MANUFACTURER
Green Chartreuse type	Anisette	A,C,B,D,E,F,H
	Anisette de Bordeaux	G,
	Apricot	B,
	Apricot Brandy	A,B,C,D,E,F,H
	Banana	G
Benedictine-type	Benedict	F
	Cacao	H
	Calisay	H
	Chartreuse	F
	Cherry	B
	Cherry Brandy	A,B,C,D,E,F,G,H
Tia Maria-type	Coffee Rum	A,B,C,D,E,F
	Cointreau	F
	Cream of Apricot	G
	Cream of Cacao	G
	Cream of Green Mint	G
	Cream of Peach	G
	Cream of Vanilla	G
	Cream of White Mint	G

TYPE	LIQUEUR	MANUFACTURER
	Creme de Menthe	A, B, C, D, E, F, H
	Creme de Moka	G
	Creme de Noyau	G
	Curacao	A, C, D, E, F, H
	Danzig	G
Benedictine-type	Dictine	A, B, C, D, E, H
	Grand Marnier	E
Green Chartreuse-type	Green Convent	G
	Green Ginger	A, B, E,
	Honey Smoke	A, B, C, D, E, F
Strega-type	Italian "S"	A
	Juniper Gin	G
	Kirsch	A, B, C, D, E, G
	Kümmel	A, C, D, E, F, G, H
	Mandarine Brandy	G
	Maraschino	A, B, C, D, E
	Mirabelle	G
	Morasquin	G
	Orange	B, F, G
	Orange Brandy	G
Cointreau-type	Orange "C"	A
Grand Marnier-type	Orange "GM"	A
	Peach	B
	Peach Brandy	A, B, C, D, E, F
	Prunelle	G
	Punch	G
	Rancio	G
	Raspberry	E
	Ratafia	G
	Red Curacao	G
Benedictine-type	Reverendine	G
	Sloe Gin	G
	Strawberry	E
	Strega	E
	Vanilla	H
	Verveine	G

	Vespetro	G
	White Curacao	G
Yellow Chartreuse-type	Yellow Convent	G

TYPE	APERITIFS & VERMOUTHS	MANUFACTURER
Aperitif	Amer	G
Italian Vermouth	Bianco	D
Aperitif	Bitter	G
Italian Vermouth	Concorrenza	D
Vermouth	Dry French	D
Vermouth	French	A, E, G
Vermouth	Italian	A, C, G
	Red Vermouth	B
	Red Wine Aperitif	G
Italian Vermouth	Torino	D
Italian Vermouth	Vermoutino Bianco	G
Aperitif	Vinquina Dore	G
Aperitif	Vinquina Gentiane	G
Aperitif	Vinquina Orange	G
Aperitif	Vinquina Rouge	G
	White Vermouth	B

KEY

SYMBOL	BRAND NAME	MANUFACTURER
A	"Winemaster"	Ritchie Products, Rollestone Road, Burton-on-Trent, Staffs. DE13 0JX.
B	"CWE"	Home Winecraft (Leicester) Ltd., 15 Viking Rd., Wigston, Leicester LE8 1BT.
C	"Leigh-Williams"	Leigh-Williams & Sons, Tattenhall, nr. Chester CH3 9PT.

D	"Vina"	Vina (Home Winemaking Supplies) Ltd., Hornby Boulevard, Bootle, Liverpool L20 5HP.
E	"Byowco"	Byowco Products Ltd., 136 Wellingborough Rd., Northampton NN1 4DT.
F	"Vinaide"	Vinaide Brewing & Food Products Ltd., 31 Blackfriars Rd., Salford, M3 5JQ.
G	"T. Noirot"	Ritchie Products (see above).
H	"Semplex"	Semplex Home Brews, Old Hall Works, Stuart Road, Birkenhead,

With the exception of the "Honey Smoke" flavouring (which I personally consider to be at its best when directly added to a straight whisky that has been sweetened to taste) the application of all the agents listed falls to a single, simple pattern. To the balance of parts listed in the Alcohol Strength Adjustment Tables B, C, and D (which, for the sake of good relations, should always be assembled in the order stated, i.e. sugar-syrup to wine and fortifying spirit to the sweetened result) they are merely added, a teaspoonful at a time, until an exploratory sip tells that all is as it should be. In the case of only a small amount of liqueur being made (and half-bottles have much to recommend them, particularly in first-instances, since they enable a selection of three or four companionable potions to be assembled on the strength of a single bottle of spirit) the flavouring may advantageously be transferred to a small dropper-bottle persuaded from the dispensary of some friendly chemist. Alternatively, it can be administered, drop by pungent drop, via a pipette (of the old-fashioned fountain-pen filler type) fitted with a rubber teat. For the flavour adjustment of 26 cc. single-glass tasting samples the flavouring is best added as a dilution, one or two drops having been spread through four or eight times their quantity of wine.

The wine used needs to be of as neutral a flavour as possible: ideally, one specifically designed to meet the needs of the purpose we have in mind for it. The end product of the Liqueur Wine-base formulation already detailed, if completely clear and stable by the time we are ready for it, must be regarded as a First Choice. In the event of this not being available, any wine (commercial or home-made) based on the fermentation of pure grape juice, "white" grape concentrate, raisins, sultanas, apples, bananas, or any of these in combination, will serve.

In all these cases the wine, varying from white to richly golden, can be considered appropriate for inclusion in the majority of liqueurs since, in the event of a red being required, a taste-free vegetable colouring can be circumspectly added. Grape wines which are themselves red through having been fermented on the skins and pulp of the fruit, or which have been produced from deliberately red grape concentrates, are not so adaptable unless one is prepared to accept a deal of licence as regards the colour of the liqueur to which they are put. If this presents no obstacle, however, there are a number of country wines the distinctive flavours of which blend well with particular essences to provide imaginative liqueurs open to the acceptance of evocative names which the producer can himself apply.

The chart that follows is for general guidance purposes only. If you would soar higher, blessings on you and may wings waft you on your pleasant way.

WINE	RESERVE FOR USE IN COMBINATION WITH
Apricot	Apricot Brandy, Creme de Noyau, French Vermouth, Italian Vermouth, Kirsch.
Bilberry	Cherry Brandy, Ratafia.
Elderberry	Cherry Brandy, Orange Brandy, Ratafia.
Gooseberry	French Vermouth, Italian Vermouth.
Greengage	French Vermouth, Italian Vermouth.
Morello Cherry	Cherry Brandy, Kirsch, Morasquin, Prunelle, Ratafia, Reverendine.

Peach	Creme de Noyau, French Vermouth, Italian Vermouth, Kirsch, Peach Brandy.
Prune	Creme de Moka, Danzig, Juniper Gin, Mandarine Brandy, Mirabelle, Morasquin, Orange Brandy, Peach Brandy, Prunelle, Punch, Ratafia, Sloe Gin, Vanilla.
Rosehip	Anisette, Apricot Brandy, Cherry Brandy, Kirsch, Mirabelle, Morasquin, Peach Brandy, Prunelle, Punch, Ratafia, Red Curacao, Reverendine, Vanilla.
Sweet Cherry	Cherry Brandy, Kirsch, Morasquin, Prunelle, Ratafia, Reverendine.
White Currant	French Vermouth, Italian Vermouth.
Yellow Plum	French Vermouth, Italian Vermouth, Mirabelle, Prunelle.

No stage of any beverage-productive process can be more open to the application of individual whims and fancies than that loosely covered by the instruction "sweeten to taste".

An average sugar content of four ounces (represented by 5 fl. oz. of a simple syrup compounded in accordance with the recommendations to be found on page 76) per bottle of liqueur has been set down as a standard for consideration. Everyone must, however, experiment and ascertain for him or herself the optimum balance of sweetness and alcohol strength commensurate to the type of product being aimed for. In this regard, liqueurs such as Anisette, Banana, Cacao, Creme de Menthe, Green Mint, Morasquin, Punch, White Mint and Vanilla are generally at their best when very sweet indeed and a sugar content as high as 12 oz. per bottle may not be considered excessive by those who enjoy a syrup consistency spiked with sufficient alcohol to offset its cloying effect. Liqueurs of Benedictine and Chartreuse type, coffee liqueurs, all the curacaos (including Grand Marnier-types), Danzig, Kummel, Vespetro and Verveine generally benefit by being fractionally less sweet (around 10 oz. of sugar per bottle).

Italian vermouths can well pack 6 oz. of sugar behind their label but only one-third of this amount (2 oz.) is adequate for the average French formulation.

The degree of sweetness appropriate to aperitifs needs to be built up according to the bittering effect of the constituents involved. Vermoutino Bianco, for example, requires no sugar at all. Both Red and White Wine Aperitifs, however, benefit by the addition of 4 oz.–6 oz. whilst the bitterest aperitifs of all (sold under proprietary names such as "Angostura", "Amara", "Campari" and "Fernet Branca") can batter a palate to insensibility unless smoothed and rounded by the influence that 10 oz. can provide.

On all occasions when such adjustments can be anticipated it is best to start by weighing out the amount of sugar to be used and relating this, by means of the following scale, to the actual volume (in terms of parts) it will occupy in relation to the Alcohol Strength Adjustment Tables provided:

WEIGHT OF SUGAR	VOLUME IN TERMS OF PARTS
2 oz	1¼
4 oz	2½
6 oz	3¾
8 oz	5
10 oz	6¼
12 oz	7½

Turning, then, to the Alcohol Strength Adjustment Tables, select the final strength appropriate to our needs. Total the number of parts advised by columns A and B and from the resultant figure deduct the volume our intended sugar addition is to occupy. The balance remaining is the volume of wine in which this needs to be dissolved, under the persuasion of gentle heat and continuous stirring. Fortification in accordance with the Table and flavour addition to taste then follows as a matter of routine.

Compared against the final alcohol strengths promised by the Tables in respect of any putting together of component parts, the results of calculations conducted as above will, in some instances, prove fractionally adrift. As a defence measure against those who seek controversy the point must also be made that in extreme cases, at either end of the sugar scale, variations up to plus or minus 3° may be experienced. This is inevitable unless one is prepared to indulge a series of mental hand-springs aimed at providing precise wine-sugar-spirit balances: an exercise not overlooked in the appendices to this volume, but one unlikely to be explored by those anxious to be formulating rather than figuring.

To these latter folk are dedicated the individual and detailed recipes that follow, starting with:

ABRICOTINE   A sweet liqueur of notably high alcohol content (in this instance 58°–61° proof according to the strength of white wine employed) laced with the decidedly almond flavour of the crushed fruit kernels. Dispensed too generously, it will be found ideal for the institution of spiritual revivals or the breaking of a lease.

Ingredients   12 oz. sugar, 9 fl. oz. of whatever white wine comes most readily to hand, 9½ fl. oz. of 140° Polish spirit, apricot flavouring, almond essence.

Method   Place the wine in a small saucepan (the smaller the better) and add the sugar. Apply the gentlest of heats, stirring continuously, until the sugar is dissolved. On no account allow the mixture to boil.

Leave the resulting syrup to cool but, whilst it is still lukewarm, add the spirit and mix well before flavouring to taste with the apricot and almond essences, the latter being dispensed drop by circumspect drop so that it provides an undertone only and never dominates the situation. A few days of maturing will assist the general effect.

AMER PICON   A popular but bitter liqueur, rarely consumed neat but frequently employed in the mixing of cocktails (which might otherwise taste too mellow) and often drunk as an aperitif when diluted: 2 oz. of the cordial to about 4 oz. of cold water. Grenadine (a heavy syrup containing a high proportion of pomegranate juice and obtainable from the specialist supplier of winemaking ingredients) is generally used for sweetening purposes.

The following formulation will provide a bottle strength of 38° proof.

124

Ingredients   2 oz. sugar, 18½ fl. oz. Liqueur Wine-base, 6 fl. oz. 68° vodka, amer extract.

Method   Gently warm the sugar into the wine-base and add the spirit when the solution is cool. Then add the amer extract to taste.

ANESONE   A superlative digestive and a sure defence against an attack of the collywobbles or anything that might go bump in the night. For a 51° proof result follow the recipe hereunder. This may, however, be modified or extended (in accordance with the Alcohol Strength Adjustment Tables) as inclination dictates.

Ingredients   5 fl. oz. of sugar-syrup, 13½ fl. oz. 21° white table wine, 7½ fl. oz. 140° polish spirit, anisette flavouring and (optionally, but it *does* give a lift to the eyebrows) peppermint essence.

Method   Add the sugar-syrup to the wine and mix well. Add the spirit and mix again. Flavour to taste, using the anisette medium, before applying the merest trace of peppermint underpinning should this be required. A bone crochet-hook, dipped lightly in the peppermint essence and then used to stir the concoction, will often be found to convey the requisite amount of minty influence.

ANISETTE DE BORDEAUX   There are many liqueurs of solid reputation based on Star Aniseed Oil: a distillate obtained from the dried fruits of the star anise illicium verum. Anisette de Bordeaux, believed by some to have been the inspiration of them all, is credited to a grandmother of Marie Brizard.

It aids the digestion, has a proper flavour for the ladies and, at its commercial strength of 44° proof, a proper authority for gentlemen. The recipe that follows has been designed to meet these requirements. In the event of any alternative strength being desired, or in the case of it being more convenient to use liquors other than those specified, reference should be made to the Alcohol Strength Adjustment Tables.

Ingredients   5 fl. oz. sugar-syrup, 8 fl. oz. Liqueur Wine-base, 13 fl. oz. 68° proof vodka, Anisette de Bordeaux extract.

Method   Add the sugar-syrup to the wine base. Mix well. Add the spirit and mix again. Finally, flavour to taste. With all this conducted to your satisfaction, a touch of green vegetable colouring will not come amiss.

APRICOT BRANDY   This is a liqueur permitted a deal of licence. It can be as gentle or assertive as one cares to make it: a point illustrated by the range of 40°–70° proof met with in the commercial product.

The recipe that follows is a middle-of-the-roader (45° proof) based on the use of a 21° white table wine (a banana wine is ideal!) and 68° vodka.

Ingredients 4 oz. of sugar, 7½ fl. oz. of wine, 15 fl. oz. 68° vodka, 1 fl. oz. pure glycerine, and apricot brandy extract or essence.

Method Dissolve the sugar in the wine under the influence of gentle heat and continuous stirring. Allow the mixture to cool and, when just lukewarm, add the spirit and then the glycerine. Finally, flavour to taste.

This is another of the liqueurs improved by a short period of maturing, so leave it for a week or so…if you can!

APRICOT SPIRITS A general term covering a variety of apricot-flavoured liqueurs fortified to a wide range of alcohol strengths by means of whatever spirit happens to be most conveniently accessible. Apricot Brandy is the one that comes most readily to mind but Apricot Gin, Apricot Vodka and Apricot Whisky all deserve to be better known. For a 40° proof Apricot Gin or Apricot Whisky blend 9 fl. oz. of a 21° proof table wine into 5 fl. oz. of sugar-syrup and fortify with 12 fl. oz. of the appropriate spirit. For an Apricot Vodka of the same final strength use only 8½ fl. oz. of the wine, 5 fl. oz. of sugar-syrup and 12½ fl. oz. of 68° vodka. For a smoother liqueur of slightly greater body, reduce the sugar-syrup by 1 fl. oz. in all cases and mix in 1 fl. oz. of glycerine immediately prior to the flavouring addition.

BENEDICTINE In spite of four-hundred-and-sixty-five years spent trying, no outsider has yet completely rumbled all the closely-guarded Benedictine secrets (around seventy-five in number) of the liqueur to which that religious Order gives its name, each bottle labelled "D.O.M." in abbreviation of the latin "Deo Optimo Maximo" (To God, the Most Good, the Most Great).

There have been several commendable near-misses (the South American "Monastique", for example) but the original formulation of the good Brother Benedict goes on defying all challenges, unique in the balance of its herb personalities. Some day, perhaps, the special magic of their influence will be revealed. Against the possibility of time hanging heavy meanwhile, the following 72° proof recipe is submitted that it might serve the function of a spiritual and physical prop.

Ingredients   8 oz. sugar, 9 fl. oz. of a well matured and preferably golden wine, 12 fl. oz. of 140° proof Polish spirit, dictine flavouring essence.

Method   Gently heat the sugar into the wine. Allow to cool and, whilst still lukewarm, incorporate the spirit. Flavour to taste.

For a less sweet end-product of identical strength, use the following alternative recipe which may, incidentally, be adjusted (in accordance with the Tables provided) to meet any specific alcohol requirement.

Ingredients   5 fl. oz. sugar-syrup, 9 fl. oz. of a well matured and preferably golden wine, 12 fl. oz. of 140° proof Polish spirit, dictine flavouring essence.

Method   Well mix the sugar-syrup into the wine. Add the spirit and mix again. Flavour to taste.

(Note: regarding the nature of the wine to be used, almost *any* mature and full-bodied wine will serve excellently. If all you happen to have in the cellar or attic is a bottle of Aunty Maggie's 1980 Broad Bean, give it a whirl!)

CHERRY BRANDY   If demand be any criterion, this is the liqueur that most suits the English palate. The method of its production by flavour addition falls to the standard pattern already emphasised by the Strength Adjustment Tables. Since, however, no collection of recipes would be complete without mention of it, here it is again: balanced, in this instance, to the popular commercial strength of 42° proof on the basis of a 21° proof full-bodied red table wine (a well matured Elderberry, one without harshness, for example) plus 68° vodka.

Ingredients   5 fl. oz. sugar-syrup, 7 fl. oz. richly-red table wine, 14 fl. oz. vodka, cherry brandy extract.

Method   Blend the sugar-syrup into the wine and add the spirit. When all are well mixed, add the flavouring to taste.

For a liqueur of additional smoothness, reduce the amount of sugar-syrup used to 4 fl. oz. and introduce 1 fl. oz. of pure glycerine to the mix prior to its flavour adjustment. Should a result of somewhat sharper edge be required, add half-a-saltspoon of citric acid and a trace of grape tannin.

CHESKY One of the lesser known cherry liqueurs, popular in Victorian times but currently out of fashion, blended (as the contrived name suggests) on a basis of whisky. "Gean" is another such, taking its title from the particular variety of white cherry commonly used in its production. Both deserve to be better known, and probably would be if honestly described as Cherry Whisky, for the flavour of cherries, like that of apricots and many other fruits, is accommodating in the extreme, lending itself admirably to a wide selection of fortifying spirits. For a 42° proof concoction you will require:

Ingredients 5 fl. oz. of sugar-syrup, 7½ fl. oz. of a full-bodied red table wine, 13½ fl. oz. of whisky and a straight cherry (as opposed to a cherry brandy) flavouring essence.

Method As for Cherry Brandy.

By making use of a commercial port or British ruby wine (already kicked to a strength of 36° proof during the course of its manufacture) a truly economic 42° liqueur results from the putting together of:

Ingredients 5 fl. oz. of sugar-syrup, 11½ fl. oz. of the commercially fortified wine, 9½ fl. oz. of 70° whisky, and cherry flavouring.

Method As for Cherry Brandy.

CREME DE MENTHE As revealed by the range of flavouring extracts and essences listed at the beginning of this chapter, there are many different brands of volatile and aromatic compounds specifically designed to meet the requirements of this popular 52° after-dinner helpmeet. Those described as Cream of White Mint and Cream of Green Mint are equally suited to the general nature of this particular liqueur, and in the event of your local wine-supplies stockist being closed when the urge to get productive is upon you, even a touch of domestic peppermint flavouring will serve to provide a very acceptable result.

Green, white, golden and even ruby colourings are appropriate by commercial standards, but if conservatively-minded dinner-guests are due to arrive the familiar green tint is the one most likely to strike a responsive chord, obviating any necessity for involved explanation.

Ingredients 12 oz. sugar, 11½ fl. oz. 32° liqueur wine-base, 7 fl. oz. 140° Polish spirit, any one of the flavourings mentioned (i.e.

crème de menthe, cream of white mint, cream of green mint, or domestic peppermint essence) and vegetable colouring.

Method Place the sugar in a small saucepan and add the liqueur wine-base. Stir well before applying gentle heat and continue stirring 'till all the sugar has dissolved. On no account allow the mixture to boil or even approach boiling temperature. Allow the resultant syrup to cool, but whilst it is still lukewarm, add the spirit and mix again before flavouring to taste. Colour as necessary when quite cold.

CRÈME DE VANILLE Another of the liqueurs well catered for in the essence-supplier's lists but one for which any good domestic vanilla essence will prove appropriate.

For an end product of 52° proof, the balance of ingredients (and the method of their involvement) should be exactly as for Crème de Menthe.

DRAMBUIDH Not a typographical error, nor a mis-spelling of the eminent Drambuie liqueur, but an apt description of what Drambuie is: an aromatised whisky.

It may be recalled that, when promising that a standard pattern of procedure might be followed in respect of all the flavouring essences listed, "Honey Smoke" was singled out as an exception to the general rule. The reason for this deviation lies in the fact that, whisky being what it is, no chance of encouraging home-grown Scotch exists. If it is to retain its essential character (born of grain and sun, peat and heather moor, the crash of waterfalls and the whisper of running brooks over smooth rocks) the commercial spirit *can* only be blended with other whiskies or be given the support of additional aromatic ethers such as those which Honey Smoke essences contain.

To convert a straight whisky to something higher (closely resembling, if not identical with, the more expensive Drambuie) it is, thus, only necessary to dissolve 2 oz. of sugar in 24¼ fl. oz. of the spirit and to flavour the result with one or two teaspoonfuls of Honey Smoke essence according to taste.

A loss of 3° proof (accounted for by the sugar addition) is inevitable. If this should really irk, however, it can be compensated for by the extra addition of half-an-ounce of Polish spirit.

MIL–5

FRAMBOISE, FRAISIA These are raspberry and strawberry-flavoured liqueurs respecitvely, both lending themselves admirably to the uncomplicated process of flavour-by-essence addition. In both cases their degree of sweetness needs to be fairly high: around 8 oz. of sugar per 26 fl. oz. bottle. This amount can, however, be incorporated without the general balance of parts recommended by the Alcohol Strength Adjustment Tables needing to be altered. Taking by way of example the production of a 45° proof end-product, you will require:

Ingredients 8 oz. of sugar, 7½ fl. oz. of liqueur wine-base, 13½ fl. oz. of 68° vodka, and raspberry or strawberry essence according to the type of liqueur required.

Method Gently warm the sugar into the wine-base 'till dissolved; then mix in the spirit and flavouring to taste.

Colouration (a delicate pink is more appropriate than a deep red) is best applied by the circumspect introduction of cochineal.

GREEN CHARTREUSE Regarded as one of the finest liqueurs, this historic potable has so many imitators that the comprehensive term "Liqueur Vert" has been deliberately coined to encompass them. Some have been acclaimed and risen to eminence in their own right; others, compared against the original and best left anonymous, stand as much chance as a crow at a party of peacocks.

The recipe presented here (braced with Polish spirit to match exactly the commercial product as regards its exceptional 96° proof strength) is submitted in the belief that it brings the amateur liqueur-maker to within a whisper of the genuine product. It is, nevertheless, a swank formulation: one that makes no concession to the average person's economic pressures of the day. A second recipe therefore follows: one adjusted to provide a completely satisfactory half-strength (48°) liqueur retaining all the nicest qualities the formidable elixir but produced on the basis of a 21° table wine (of minimum colour) and 68° vodka.

Provided that the sugar content per 26 fl. oz. bottle is allowed to remain as 8 oz. in all cases, any number of further strength variations can, of course, be arranged in accordance with the Tables provided.

Recipe No. 1.

Ingredients 8 oz. sugar, 4 fl. oz. 32° liqueur wine-base, 17 fl. oz.

polish spirit, Green Convent liqueur flavouring, green colouring matter.

Method Start by facing the relatively minor problem of persuading a fairly large amount of sugar to completely dissolve in a comparatively small volume of liquor. This is best achieved by introducing the sugar to the wine-base in two separate quantities, the second addition not being made until the first (influenced by gentle warmth and continuous stirring) has fallen to a syrup state.

When all the sugar has been incorporated, and the resultant heavy syrup shows no trace of solid material, the mix is allowed to cool, the spirit being stirred in whilst the concoction is still lukewarm. The requisite flavouring and colouring are then added, the latter being dispensed to provide the degree of shade latched on to by polite society's most with-it interior decorators.

Recipe No. 2.

Ingredients 8 oz. sugar, 5 fl. oz. table wine, 16 fl. oz. vodka, Green Convent liqueur flavouring extract, green wine-and-spirit colouring.

Method As for Recipe No. 1.

MANDARINE No mention has yet been made of any recipe incorporating brandy as the source of its compelling influence. This liqueur, rich with the after-dinner Christmas flavour of small deep-coloured oranges, makes it possible to remedy the deficiency. The final strength aimed for in the balance of parts quoted hereunder (42°) is a for-instance rather than a particular recommendation since it is believed that the reader will, by now, be well aware of the possibilities open to him, and how he may juggle this and that to obtain any result he specifically desires.

Ingredients 8 oz. of sugar, 7½ fl. oz. of a full-bodied 21° table wine, 13½ fl. oz. of 70° brandy, Mandarine Brandy flavouring.

Method Warm and stir the sugar into the wine to produce a thin syrup. Allow to cool but, whilst it is still lukewarm, add the spirit. Flavour to taste.

For an interesting variation well worth serious consideration, use whisky in place of brandy on a volume-for-volume basis.

MONASTINE This French liqueur, devised by the Brothers of the Abbaye St. Gratien, is so reminiscent of 75° proof Yellow Chartreuse as to be virtually identical with the latter product.

That is a personal opinion and we will be damned for it. In any case, there can be no good reason for picking upon one of two such closely related liqueurs in the discussion of a type. For the production of an intensely aromatic cordial closely resembling either or both and reaching to within decimal points of their commercial strength take, therefore:

Ingredients   10 oz. sugar, 7¾ fl. oz. of 32° liqueur wine-base, 12 fl. oz. Polish spirit, Yellow Convent liqueur extract, golden wine-and-spirit colouring.

Method   As for Green Chartreuse.

For an end result of any lesser strength, follow the recommendations of the Alcohol Strength Adjustment Tables (using a well-matured and richly-golden table wine should this be available) but in all cases substitute 8 oz. of sugar for the quantity of sugar-syrup advised. Methods as for Framboise and Fraisia.

Chapter VIII

Some Further Cordial Relationships

THE recipes that follow, alphabetically assembled and classified as to type wherever possible, are of a very general nature. Here and there you will find suggestions for flavoursome alcoholic beverages that are not strictly liqueurs at all. These have won their place merely because they are nice to have around.

In all cases the balance of parts detailed are recommendations only, to be ignored or modified as inclination dictates. You, the reader, are bound by one obligation only, and that to your own palate. In setting out to accumulate a variety of practical adjuncts to your living, not merely a hobby for exhibition to your friends, look first to your own needs.

One word of warning before we explore the new territory: spread the sampling over a long period. Scheherazade, we are told, beguiled her Sultan for a thousand and one nights to win her ultimate reward. Be well advised to spin your own tale as softly and lovingly.

Who wants to be carried around in a basket, anyway!

ADVOCAAT Sometimes spelled "Advockaat" and classified as an emulsion liqueur. A typical Netherlands composition for the dyking of the human system against the ills and chills of an inclement climate.

Traditionally of a slow-pouring and gurgle-inducing thickness, cream, condensed milk and all manner of body-building ingredients are to be found listed in many easily available recipes. These, however, we shall ignore since the consistency of an authentic product lies in the method by which its egg-yolks, sugar and aromatic spirits are blended together "au bain-marie": a term indicating the use of a double saucepan or boiler (easily improvised by placing a bowl within a second vessel containing hot water).

At a particular temperature the mixture begins to emulsify (i.e. the various ingredients mix but do not dissolve) and it is then cooled as rapidly as possible.

Ingredients The yolks of fifteen eggs, 17½ oz. of granulated sugar, 26 fl. oz. 70° proof brandy, the seed from one vanilla pod and a pinch of salt.

Method Prepare a bain-marie by setting an empty bowl in a pan of not-too-vigorously boiling water. Whisk the egg-yolks, vanilla seed, sugar and salt together until the combination is thick and frothy: then add the brandy (but slowly, slowly, slowly), whisking all the time.

When all is assembled, transfer the mixture to the heated bowl of the improvised bain-marie, continuing to whisk rapidly 'till all is thick. Then very quickly transfer the heated bowl to a depth of cold water (iced, if possible) so that the liqueur may be rapidly cooled to prevent its curdling.

When all is safely bottled and corked, relax for two months whilst things mature.

This recipe will provide two bottles of a 35° proof liqueur considerably stronger and of more body than the commercial preparation frequently encountered and which, on being sampled by a Dutchman of strong opinions, merely evoked the request that someone should pass him a nipple!

ANGELICA Classed as a herb liqueur produced, in this instance, by a process of maceration. Although the name is taken from the principal ingredient involved, the commercial product (hailing from the Basque region of Spain) is additionally flavoured with certain aromatic plants found in the Pyrenees. The 41° proof formulation that follows dispenses with these and is, to that extent, a simplification. Sweetness is an essential characteristic of this liqueur and is well catered for by the amount of sugar recommended in the recipe. This amount can, however, be cut by half to meet individual requirements, and the final strength of the concoction can be reduced or extended in accordance with the recommendations of Strength Adjustment Tables B, and C.

Ingredients 8 oz. sugar, 11 fl. oz. 32° liqueur wine-base, 10 fl. oz. 70° brandy, 1 oz. of stem angelica, 1 oz. of bitter almonds.

Method Blanch the almonds and coarse chop them. Measure the spirit into a screw-topped jar and add the almonds and angelica, leaving both these to soak for seven days. At the end of this period, place the sugar in a small saucepan and pour on the liqueur wine-base. Stir well before applying gentle warmth and continue stirring until a clear and virtually colourless syrup results. Allow to cool to lukewarm: then strain the flavoured spirit into it.

This liqueur will continue to improve the longer it is kept.

ANIS Classified as a seed liqueur, this is a blatant Spanish and Latin-American copy of Anisette but is usually somewhat sweeter. The recipe that follows is, therefore, an adaptation of that provided in Chapter VII, allowing for the inclusion of twice the amount of sugar (8 oz.) whilst retaining a target of 44° proof.

Ingredients 8 oz. sugar, 6 fl. oz. of a white table wine, 15 fl. oz. 68° vodka, Anisette flavouring, green vegetable colouring.

Method Completely dissolve the sugar in the wine, applying a minimum amount of heat and stirring continuously. Cool to just lukewarm. Add the spirit and flavour to taste. Colour as necessary.

ARRAC PUNSCH A Scandinavian liqueur taking its name, for the most part, from the Arabic word "arak" which originally meant "sweat" or "juice" but which, in various forms, is current throughout Asia to mean spirits. These, in Europe at least, are usually distilled from rice and molasses, the latter imparting a rum-like flavour. It is not, therefore, surprising that the best arrac comes from the East Indies ("Batavian Arrack") and Jamaica.

The recipe that follows, fortified up to 83° proof by means of rum and Polish spirit in combination, packs a wallop quite capable of unhooking Father Christmas' whiskers at three paces. It should, therefore, be approached with respect and consideration for the neighbours.

Ingredients 5 fl. oz. sugar-syrup, 4 fl. oz. 21° white table wine (one based on barley or wheat for preference), 5 fl. oz. 80° rum, 12 fl. oz. Polish spirit, anisette essence.

Method Add the sugar-syrup to the wine and mix well. Add the rum and mix again. Add the Polish spirit and give a final stir before flavouring with two teaspoonfuls of the essence.

ATHOL BROSE Classified for the sake of simplicity as a compounded beverage, there are many Schools of Thought regarding the proper construction of this Scottish National Spine Stiffener. Any recipe is, thus, open to critcism: bound to cause controversy. Let us, however, ignore the volleying and thundering and stick our necks out to the extent of:

Ingredients 3 heaped dessertspoonfuls of porridge oats (*not* the "instant" kind), 8 oz. of cream, 2 dessertspoons of liquid honey, 8 fl. oz. of whisky, and 3 dessertspoons of sherry.

Method To the oats add just sufficient water to cover and leave to soak overnight. Transfer to a small muslin or nylon straining bag and squeeze the liquor into a large jug. To this now add the cream, stirring well to ensure its proper involvement. Next add the whisky and stir again before pouring in the sherry. Finally add the honey and go at the whole assemblage with a fork (or, preferably, some patent whisking gadget) to ensure that the honey does not sink to a layer at the bottom of the other combined ingredients.

Bottle, cork and leave to mature for five days in a refrigerator, taking it out to thaw a little an hour or so before it is required.

(Note: Athol Brose is best served from a bowl and should be well stirred from time to time prior to and during its being ladled out. Note also: it will not keep indefinitely and is at its best when made specially to meet the demands of some particular occasion).

BADIANE Classified as a herb liqueur (35° proof) and produced by a simple maceration process.

Ingredients 8 oz. sugar, 13 fl. oz. 70° brandy, 9 whole cloves, 1 stick of cinnamon, 1 oz. of blanched almonds, lemon essence.

Method Soak the cloves, cinnamon and blanched almonds in the spirit 'till their flavour influence is clearly evident to the palate. Filter.

Place the sugar in a saucepan and pour on 8 fl. oz. of water. Bring to a gentle simmer, stirring all the while, 'till a clear and virtually colourless syrup results. Cool to lukewarm and then add the spirit. Finally add one or two drops of lemon essence to taste.

BLACKBERRY BRANDY A fruit liqueur based on berries collected from the prickly bushes or brambles of a plant belonging to the Rosaceae family; deliberately cropped in many countries but growing wild throughout the world and particularly lushful in the Northern Hemisphere.

The following recipe, employing the process of juice and flavour extraction by the use of enzymes, provides a final strength of 40° proof.

Ingredients 1 lb. Blackberries, 4 oz. sugar, 2 fl. oz. 70° brandy, 6½ fl. oz. Polish spirit.

Method   Pick the fruit over for any stalks, leaves or unsound berries which may be present and leave to soak for fifteen minutes in a salt solution. Transfer to a colander and rinse, gently but thoroughly, in cold water. Put in a basin and crush before adding half-a-teaspoon each of Rohament P and some anti-pectin enzyme. Stir well, cover the basin with a clean cloth and place it in a warm atmosphere (perhaps the spare corner of an airing-cupboard).

After twenty-four hours transfer the resulting purée to a saucepan and bring to a simmering temperature of 66°–72° Centigrade (151°–162° Fahrenheit). Then, whilst it is still hot, place the purée in a scalded jelly-bag or several thicknesses of fine muslin and strain, applying hand pressure as soon as the cooling slop permits. Leave for an hour or so during which time a small deposit may have formed. Should this be so, be careful to pour off only the clear juice, measuring 15 fl. oz. of this into a small saucepan. In the event of the juice quantity not being sufficient, top up to the required volume with a red table-wine. Add the sugar, stir and apply just enough warmth to produce a clear syrup.

Allow to cool before mixing in the brandy followed by the Polish spirit.

COFFEE RUM   Classed as a seed liqueur, the description "Coffee Rum" covers a wide range of distinctly similar concoctions individually known as Crème de Cafe, Crème de Mocca, Kahlua, Tia Maria and so on, their principal differences being the degree of sweetness associated with them. The recipe given here is, therefore, of a somewhat general character.

Prevented as we are from the employment of distillation techniques, the higher commercial strengths (around 55° proof) are not within amateur reach since the use of sufficient fortifying spirit for their attainment would necessitate the loss of a more important flavour balance. A 42° end product is, however, powerful enough to satisfy the majority of requirements.

Ingredients   8 oz. soft brown sugar, 10 fl. oz. of black coffee, 5 fl. oz. 80° rum, 5 oz. 140° Polish spirit, 1 oz. glycerine, vanilla essence, coffee-rum flavouring.

Method   Make half-a-pint of black coffee using a good blend of freshly ground beans. Whilst it is still hot strain it through several thicknesses of fine muslin on to the sugar, stirring 'till this is completely dissolved. Allow to cool, then stir in the rum and polish spirit. Add half-a-teaspoon of vanilla essence, the glycerine and coffee-rum flavouring to taste. Mix well and bottle.

CRÈME DE CASSIS A fruit liqueur and one of several principally flavoured with the soft and velvety influence of blackcurrants, the juice of which, weight for weight, contains double the quantity of Vitamin C as does that of fresh oranges. The recipe quoted thus provides, in addition to its 42° proof companionship, as nice a means of stacking up general health resources as any yet hit upon by those inclined to take a little something for medicinal reasons.

The method employed involves the use of enzyme additives.

Ingredients In addition to Rohament P and an anti-pectin: 4 oz. sugar, 8 oz. blackcurrants, 8½ fl. oz. of 21° red table wine, 5 oz. 70° brandy, 4 oz. 140° Polish spirit, 1 fl. oz. glycerine.

Method Remove stems and calyces from the fruit which should be placed in a bowl and crushed with a fork or the back of a kitchen spoon. Pour on the wine and stir well before adding half-a-teaspoon each of Rohament P and the anti-pectin. Stir again, cover the bowl with a clean cloth and place in a warm atmosphere (ideally around 70° Fahrenheit).

Leave for twenty-four hours. At the end of this time, transfer the wine-and-fruit purée to a scalded jelly-bag (or several thicknesses of fine muslin) and strain it, as hot as possible, into a glass jug.

During the course of the next hour or so a fine deposit may form. Measure 13½ fl. oz. of the clear liquid into a small saucepan and add the sugar. Stir and apply the minimum heat necessary to ensure that the sugar is completely dissolved, then allow to cool prior to involving the brandy and polish spirit. Finally, mix in the glycerine.

CURACAO Once used to identify a specific liqueur (made in the seventeenth century from the dried peel of unripe-green oranges brought back by Dutch traders visiting the island of Curacao in the Netherlands Antilles) the word "Curacao" is now employed as a general term classifying a wide range of peel liqueurs principally flavoured with the oils of orange fruits.

The Dutch liqueur distilleries showed great interest in these aromatic substances from the start. The rest of the world quickly latched on and to-day curacaos are the product of many countries. Variations, of course, abound; not only in respect of colour (introduced by means of vegetable dyes) but also on account of the type of orange used. Sevilles, Valencias, tangerines, mandarins, naartjies: all have a quota of some distinctive influence to offer, whilst the use of West Indian brown in place of white sugar often provides a further flavour difference.

Some of the curacao liqueurs have developed such reputations in their own right that the general term applicable to them now pales to insignificance. Cointreau and Grand Marnier are typical examples of superlative elixirs that have grown away from their parent group to achieve particular sophistication. A good home-made curacao is not, however, difficult to achieve and one might, indeed, do worse than become hooked on this particular aspect of liqueur production, experimenting with the use of different base-wines, different spirits and different sugars. The recipes that follow (starting with the simplest of all and leading through to a classical Van der Hum, the formulation of which is set out towards the end of this chapter) will serve as a guide well worth heeding.

Recipe No. 1. Final Strength: 52° proof. Flavour by addition.

Ingredients 5 fl. oz. sugar-syrup, 2 fl. oz. 32° liqueur wine-base, 19 fl. oz. 68° vodka and any one of the following extracts or essences: Orange, Orange "C", Orange "GM", Cointreau, Curacao, Grand Marnier. Colouring as required.

Method Blend the liqueur wine-base and sugar-syrup together. Add the spirit and flavour to taste. Make colourful with vegetable dye as inclination dictates.

Recipe No. 2. Final Strength: 67° proof. Flavour by maceration/ addition.

Ingredients 5 fl. oz. sugar-syrup, 10 fl. oz. 21° white table wine, 11 fl. oz. Polish spirit, the peel of one large orange (if there are areas of unripe green, so much the better) and any one of the orange flavourings listed in Recipe No. 1.

Method Carefully grate the orange peel (painstakingly excluding all white pith which has an unwanted bittering effect) and leave this to soak in the spirit for two days. Mix the sugar-syrup into the wine and into the resulting dilution strain the now flavoured spirit through filter paper or a paper towel to remove any small solid particles of matter or excess oil. Finally add flavouring to taste and colour as thought necessary.

Recipe No. 3. Final Strength: 54° proof. Flavour by maceration only.

Ingredients   6 oz. sugar, 3¼ fl. oz. of a 21° richly-golden table wine, 19 fl. oz. of 70° brandy or whisky according to taste, 3 large oranges.

Method   By means of a very sharp knife, slice wafer-thin petals of yellow outer surface from the peel of the oranges, rigorously avoiding any of the white pith. Transfer these fragments to a wide-mouthed jar and pour on the spirit. Close tightly and leave the peel to soak for several days or until it acquires a translucence. When this point is reached, filter the flavoured spirit to remove all solid materials and any excess oil which may be present.

By the application of gentle warmth and by means of continuous stirring, dissolve the sugar in the wine. Allow to cool and add the clear spirit.

Bottle, seal and allow to mature for at least one month. During this aging period a fine, white sediment may be thrown down. Should this happen, decant the liqueur before re-bottling or serving.

Recipe No. 4. Final Strength: not less than 35° proof. Flavour by maceration only.

Ingredients   2½ oz. sugar, 13 fl. oz. whisky, 2 oranges, 1 lemon, 1 seville orange.

Method   Using a sharp knife, "skim" the yellow outer surface from the peel of one orange (*not* the Seville) and place it in a two-pound jar fitted with a screw cap. Peel the rest of the fruits and carefully remove any trace of white pith. Transfer to a bowl and crush very thoroughly before adding to the shavings in the jar. Top off the pulped materials with the sugar and pour on the spirit.

Cap the jar tightly and leave it in a cool, dark place for seven days, giving it a shake each day or as often as possible. At the end of this time strain the liquor (by means of a scalded jelly-bag or several thicknesses of fine muslin) into a second well-sterilised jar. Again cap tightly and leave to clear. When this point is reached, siphon the liqueur off any deposit which may have formed into a 26 fl. oz. bottle. Should it be found necessary to top up with additional liquid, use a well-matured white wine fermented, if possible, on a basis of wheat or barley.

DAMSON GIN   It was a great day for the Dutch when, over three-hundred years ago, a certain professor Sylvius discovered what the aromatic juniper berry could do for a slug of raw alcohol.

There is a certain amount of disagreement as to where the inspiration came from. Some say that the good professor was working blind at the time, seeking a water-substitute to be carried on ships of the Dutch navy against the possibility of drought. Others suggest that he took a lead from the Count de Morret, a son of Henry of Navarre (he was careless that way) who had worked out something called juniper wine. Be that as it máy, the combination of spirit and plant was named Genièvre in honour of the berry. Word quickly got around and British troops returning from the Dutch wars quickly corrupted the continental involvement of genièvre to the English simplicity of gin.

Since those days the name has frequently been misapplied. As late as the last century practically every drink in Holland was called gin and neutral spirits, no matter what their principal flavouring constituent might be, continue to be known by the same term. We have, therefore, an established precedent for the use of Polish spirit in the recipe that follows and may, by following the balance of parts advised in the Alcohol Strength Adjustment Table A, obtain a 43° proof product retaining the maximum richness of the fruit involved.

Ingredients   1 lb. damsons, 4 oz. sugar, 8 fl. oz. 140° Polish spirit, almond essence, Rohament P and a quantity of some anti-pectin enzyme.

Method   Remove any stalks and rinse the fruit under a cold tap. Dry with a paper towel, wiping away the bloom common to plums of all varieties, and lightly crush by means of a heavy kitchen fork or the back of a wooden spoon. Pour off a little of the free juice and in this dissolve one Campden Tablet prior to adding half-a-teaspoon each of Rohament P and an anti-pectin. Stir well and return to the pulp. Stir again before covering the vessel with a clean cloth and placing it in a warm atmosphere for twenty-four hours. At the end of this time, transfer the resulting purée to a small saucepan and bring it to a simmering temperature of 66°–72° Centigrade (151°–162° Fahrenheit). Immediately pour it into a scalded jelly-bag, directing the clear juice into a graduated measure. The volume of this required is 15½ fl. oz. and one may well feel disposed to apply considerable hand pressure. This, however, is a temptation to be avoided. In the event of there being an insufficiency of juice, it is far better to make up the required volume using a red table wine. To the 15½ fl. oz. of juice add the sugar, dissolving this under the influence of gentle warmth and continuous stirring. The resulting volume of syrup should now read 18 fl. oz., but in the event of any variation a suitable adjustment can be made from whatever excess juice is available or by means of a further red wine addition. When the syrup is quite cold, add the spirit followed by one or two drops of the almond essence: just sufficient to apply the required undertone.

DANZIG A herb liqueur which, since the zest of oranges is evident in its formulation, could be roughly classified as one of the select curacaos. On the other hand, the flurry of gold specks associated with it (not enough to influence the rate of exchange but impressive for all that!) places it fairly and squarely with the somewhat ostentatious "gold" and "silver" elixirs dreamed up by the ancient alchemists and once thought to possess medicinal qualities of particular virtue.

A substantial bitterness is evident in the formulation and a fairly high sugar content (10 oz.) is necessary to adjust this to the average unsophisticated palate. The degree of sweetness which this amount provides is, however, offset by the 70° proof strength of the end product.

Ingredients 10 oz. sugar, 8¾ fl. oz. 32° liqueur wine-base, 11 fl. oz. 140° Polish spirit, Danzig flavouring extract.

Method Thoroughly dissolve the sugar in the liqueur wine-base, applying the minimum degree of heat necessary to effect this result. Cool the syrup to lukewarm before before blending in the flavouring extract which should be well shaken, prior to its addition, so as to ensure that its entire gold-fleck content is transferred for subsequent swank purposes.

EGG BRANDY Oftimes referred to as Egg-flip or Egg-nog, this is best classified as a composed emulsive drink. Not a true liqueur within the real meaning of that term it does, however, edge closely to the outer fringe of liqueurs in general and, chiefly because of its egg content, frequently strays across the border in the guise of an Advocaat which it is not. The main difference lies in the manner of its preparation (extented whipping sessions with nary a bain-marie in sight) and the variety of its spirituous under-pinnings: brandy, rum and, less frequently, apple jack or whisky.

The addition of milk or cream to the basic ingredients is a choice offered by some recipes, but one must be careful to avoid an excessively thin end product. The recipe given below (approximately 28° proof) will serve 5–6 guests most generously. If, for the sake of convenience, it is assembled several days before required it will keep perfectly if stored in an air-tight glass jar parked on the shelf of a refrigerator or even a pantry window-sill.

Ingredients 6 fresh eggs, 1½ oz. granulated sugar, 8 fl. oz. 70° brandy, 4 fl. oz. 80° rum, 8 fl. oz. milk, 4 fl. oz. double-cream, half a grated nutmeg.

Method Separate the yolks from the whites of the eggs and, putting the whites aside for a moment, beat the yolks strenuously whilst slowly adding the sugar. Continue to thrash the mixture until all the sugar is entirely dissolved and then, but very slowly, pour in the brandy (a good one: economise at this point by using industrial waste from the Cognac region and everyone will hate your for ever!).

Follow the brandy with the rum. Should a preliminary sniff at the rum bottle have indicated that its contents are likely to take over and boss the situation, a ½ or 1 fl. oz. reduction of the suggested amount, balanced by an equivalent increase in the quantity of brandy used, will adjust matters satisfactorily. Now stir in the milk and cream, the latter whipped or as it comes in the carton. Since the thickened product makes the result of its addition a bit rich, the untumbled version is preferable to many palates.

Clean off the egg-whisking equipment and go at the whites until they will stand in peaks without hitching, then fold them into the general mixture along with the grated nutmeg.

ELIXIR D'ANVERS A herb liqueur so closely following the pattern set by the better-known Yellow Chartreuse that the two are well-nigh indistinguishable to all but the most erudite and discriminating palates. For a 74° proof product that is, therefore, remarkably similar to both take:

Ingredients 8 oz. sugar, 8 fl. oz. 32° liqueur wine-base, 12 fl. oz. 140° Polish spirit, 1 fl. oz. pure glycerine, Yellow Convent flavouring extract, yellow vegetable colouring.

Method Completely dissolve the sugar in the liqueur wine-base, stirring and applying such gentle heat as may be necessary. Cool to just lukewarm before adding the spirit, mix well, and flavour to taste. Finally, involve the glycerine and a discreet amount of colouring matter for the sake of appearances.

FRAMBOISE A fruit liqueur (43° proof in this instance) dominated by the flavour of crushed raspberries.

Ingredients 1 lb raspberries, 4 oz. sugar, 8 fl. oz. Polish spirit, half-teaspoon Rohament P, half-teaspoon anti-pectin enzyme.

Method Pick the fruit over and remove the calyces. Put in a basin and crush lightly before adding the enzymes. Stir well, cover with a clean cloth and place in a warm atmosphere (70° Fahrenheit) for a few hours or until a loose purée results. Transfer this to a small saucepan and bring to a simmering temperature of 66°–72° Centigrade (151°–162° Fahrenheit), then strain the hot juice (through a scalded jelly-bag or several thicknesses of fine muslin) into a glass vessel which will reveal any deposit formed during the next sixty minutes.

Measure off 15½ fl. oz. of the clear juice, topping up with a red table wine should this adjustment be necessary, and add the sugar. Stir and apply gentle warmth until a syrup results. Allow to cool before blending in the Polish spirit.

IRISH COFFEE The Irish are alcohol absorbers of heroic mould and it is, in consequence, natural that upon them rests the credit for three of the greatest drinks in the world. Their whiskey is worth getting to know. Of all slanders, none is less tainted with fact than the Spud legend relative to Celtic liquor. Irish whiskey is definitely *not* of mashed-potato parentage! No one with any sense will be drawn into an argument as to whether or not its *better* than Scotch. It's different and a lot of folk like both.

Cognac brandy owes somewhat to the "wild geese" and, indeed, one of the finest blends is still made by a family with a very Irish name. The finest black beer in the world brings the score to two-and-a-half, and as for the balance: ask anyone who has experienced the warm, fragrant glow that follows a cup of Irish Coffee.

If you have a moment, try this:

Into a pre-warmed stemmed-glass pour a cup of very black and very hot coffee. Add sugar to taste, 1½ fl. oz. of Irish, and top off with a sizeable dollop of whipped cream.

There you have a drink fit for an Irish king!

JAMBAVA A fruit liqueur based upon the maceration of sound ripe plums in brandy. For a 40° proof result you will require:

Ingredients   6 oz. sugar, 12 oz. plums, 15 fl. oz. 70° brandy, Prunelle flavouring extract (to be used, as necessary, for boosting purposes), plus half-a-teaspoon of Rohament P and a teaspoonful of some anti-pectin enzyme.

Method   By means of a paper towel wipe the fruit clear of any bloom that may appear upon it. Hand crush and place in a basin. Select three or four of the plum stones and crack these before returning them to the pulped mass. Now pour off a small quantity of the free juice and in this dissolve one Campden Tablet before adding the enzymes. Stir well and return the treated juice to the contents of the basin. Mix, cover the basin with a clean cloth and place it in a warm atmosphere (70° Fahrenheit) for twenty-four hours. At the end of this time transfer the resulting purée to a saucepan and heat to 66°–72° Centigrade (151°–162° Fahrenheit). Strain, whilst still hot, through a jelly-bag or several thicknesses of fine muslin, allowing the juice to drain naturally rather than under the influence of pressure. A fine deposit may settle during the course of the next hour or so. Carefully siphon or pour the clear juice off this and measure 7¼ fl. oz. into a saucepan. Add the sugar and dissolve this in the juice by means of continuous stirring and whatever amount of heat is necessary to produce a syrup. Allow to cool before adding the brandy. Should any flavour boost be required, add the Prunelle flavouring extract according to taste.

KIRSCH   Although generally considered as one of the many cherry-based fruit liqueurs extant Kirsch, of markedly almond flavour and dependent for this upon the stones rather than the juice and flesh of the fruit, fits more correctly into the "seed liqueur" category.

In order to reproduce the frequently colourless commercial product as closely as possible, the 42° proof formulation that follows suggests the use of 32° liqueur wine-base. In the event of this not being available, choose a table wine of as pale a colour as possible and replace the polish spirit with 68° vodka in accordance with the recommendations of Alcohol Strength Adjustment Table "B"

Ingredients   5 fl. oz. sugar-syrup, 17 fl. oz. 32° liqueur wine-base, 4 fl. oz. Polish spirit, Kirsch flavouring.

Method   Add the sugar-syrup to the liqueur wine-base and mix. Add the spirit and mix again. Flavour to taste.

MIL–6

KUMMEL   A herb liqueur (chiefly flavoured with caraway, orris and cumin: a plant resembling fennel) commercially produced in Holland, Germany, Russia and, indeed, all the colder countries where men need to meet nature in the raw.

The 68° proof version detailed below provides an effective counter-blast to the ills and chills of winter weather wherever it may be encountered.

Ingredients   8 oz. sugar, 8¾ fl. oz. 21° white wine, 11¼ oz. 140° Polish spirit, 1 fl. oz. Glycerine, Kümmel flavouring.

Method   Make a syrup by dissolving the sugar into the wine. Mix in the Polish spirit followed by the glycerine. Flavour to taste.

MANDARINE   At Schiedam in Holland, along the bank of the River Maas (close to the spot from which a boatload of Pilgrim Fathers set sail for the New World in 1620) there is produced a favourite eating-drink called Boeren Jongen ("Farmer Lads") or Boeren Meisjes ("Farmer Lassies") according to whether or not the raisins employed are with or without seeds. Which ever they be, these are soused in a flavoured spirit and served in a stemmed glass which one attacks with a tiny spoon (not much bigger than a salt-spoon), dipping out the plumped morsels one by one: sucking and munching. This splendid way of whiling away a Christmas afternoon becomes particularly memorable if the steeping is done in a Mandarine liqueur.

For the putting-together of a suitable recipe (42° proof strength and scaled down, as regards its sugar content, to allow for the natural sweetness of the raisins) you will need:

Ingredients   2½ fl. oz. sugar-syrup, 11½ fl. oz. 21° wine (orange, lemon and even well-matured elderberry wines can be used to advantage), 12 fl. oz. 70° brandy, Mandarine Brandy extract.

Method   Involve the sugar-syrup with the wine, mix in the brandy and flavour to taste. In the event of the liqueur not being required for raisin-sousing purposes, double the amount of sugar-syrup suggested and reduce the volume of wine by 2½ fl. oz. to produce a liqueur of 40° strength.

MARASCHINO   Classified as a fruit liqueur: a cherry brandy of distinctive flavour made at Zadar, in Dalmatia, on a basis of ripe maraska cherries. Its colour may be appropriately red or, on the other hand, it may be colourless. In both cases it is exceptionally sweet, often being used in compounded drinks in place of sugar or sugar-syrup. The recipe for a 55° proof "white" version of full commercial strength consists of:

Ingredients   10 oz. sugar, 12¼ fl. oz. 32° liqueur wine-base, 7½ fl. oz. 140° polish spirit, and Maraschino flavouring essence. In the event of a "red" liqueur being required, vegetable colouring can, of course, be applied.

Method   Place the sugar in a small saucepan and pour on the liqueur wine-base. Stir well before applying gentle heat to produce a clear syrup. Allow to cool, then mix in the spirit and flavour according to taste.

MIRABELLE   One of the "great" plum brandies, the term "brandy" being a misnomer in this instance since the liqueur is based on a colourless spirit commercially distilled from the fruit. In the interests of verisimiltude, therefore, the recipe that follows employs 32° wine-base and Polish spirit to produce a final and virtually colourless concoction of 69° proof. Should a slight tint of yellow be required this may, of course, be added by means of a vegetable dye.

Ingredients   5 fl. oz. sugar-syrup, 10½ fl. oz. liqueur wine-base, 10½ fl. oz. 140° Polish spirit, Mirabelle flavouring extract.

Method   Combine the sugar-syrup with the wine base before stirring in the polish spirit and flavouring to taste.

PEACH BRANDY   A fruit liqueur commercially produced by (1) the addition of peach flavouring essences to a quantity of spirit or (2) the maceration of peaches and their crushed stones in brandy.

Both methods are open to amateur employment. The first needs no further explanation since it is covered by the recommendations of the Alcohol Strength Adjustment Tables already provided. As regards the second, this lends itself admirably to the application of a treatment based on the use of Rohament P and anti-pectin enzymes. For the production of a 48° proof end product you will require:

Ingredients   6 sound ripe peaches, 4 oz. castor sugar, 4 oz. brown sugar, 6 fl. oz. 70° brandy, 6 fl. oz. 140° Polish spirit, and one or two drops of almond essence plus half-a-teaspoon of Rohament P and a teaspoonful of an anti-pectin.

Method   Place the fruits in a muslin bag and plunge them into boiling water. Allow to remain for thirty seconds before transferring them to cold water. This procedure will release the skins which may, then, be peeled off without difficulty. Crush by hand into a basin, add the enzymes and stir thoroughly before covering with a clean cloth. Leave in a warm atmosphere (70° Fahrenheit) for 12–24 hours. Strain off the juice through several thicknesses of fine muslin or other suitable material, allowing the purée to drain naturally.

When 9 fl. oz. of the juice has been achieved (and in the event of this quantity not being available it is far better to top-up with water rather than succumb to the temptation of applying pressure to the pulp) pour it into a saucepan and raise it to a simmering temperature of 66°–72° Centigrade (151°–162° Fahrenheit). Remove from the source of heat and stir in the castor and brown sugars 'till these are thoroughly dissolved.

Allow to cool thoroughly before adding the brandy and Polish spirit. Leave for one or two hours so that any solid material may settle as a deposit, then strain through a paper towel before applying the final touch of an almond undertone by means of the essence.

SCHILLETJE   One of many popular and long-established Dutch "peel" liqueurs developed from a recipe which took the form of allowing some lemon peel to soak in genever gin. "Fladderak" is an alternative name for this product which, except for its degree of sweetness, could be classified as a Lemon Gin.

The following recipe, almost exactly following the original concept, provides an end product of 63° proof.

Ingredients   4 oz. castor sugar, the peel of four lemons, 23½ fl. oz. of gin.

Method   By means of a very sharp knife, slice wafer-thin petals of yellow outer surface from the lemon peels, carefully avoiding any of the white pith which would induce an unpleasant bitterness. Place the cuttings in a wide-mouth screw-capped jar and pour on the spirit. Cap tightly and leave the peel shavings to steep for several days or until they acquire a transparent look.

Using coffee filter papers or a paper towel, strain the now flavoured gin on to the sugar. Stir or shake vigorously to produce a clear solution. A fine sediment may develop, in which case a further filtering should be undertaken.

SLOE GIN   Commercially prepared from sloeberries by intensive infusion and the addition of a distillate of juniper berries, this is a tart, savoury and highly flavoured fruit liqueur with a characteristic dry taste. The home-produced version is a gin made as English dry in which plumlets of the astringent blackthorn fruits are steeped for two months in order to provide a maroon shade and special flavour appreciated by discriminating palates over many centuries. Economy is, thus, only one attraction of the following 45° proof formulation.

Ingredients 5 fl. oz. sugar-syrup, 1 lb. sloes, 8 fl. oz. liqueur wine-base, 13 fl. oz. of gin, and 6 blanched bitter almonds, finely minced, *or* a small eggspoon of almond essence.

Method Rinse the fruit in cold water and wipe dry, then well bruise it and place it in a wide-necked screw-capped jar. Add the minced almonds (or almond essence) and pour on the gin. Mix thoroughly and leave for at least two months, under tight seal, with occasional shakings.

At the end of the two-month period, strain the liquor through several thicknesses of fine muslin.

Combine the sugar-syrup with the liqueur wine-base, then add the flavoured gin.

USQUEBAUGH PUNCH There are two queries attached to this label. Irish tradition states without equivocation that the designation "usquebaugh" had its origins in the word "uisgebetha" and purists of the tribe go so far as to state firmly that it was invented by the glorious St. Patrick himself, so it was, whilst the sweet gentleman was resting from his snake-chasing labours and other good deeds. Scotch historians beg to differ and dourly note that the word was "uisgebah" as any bairn knows. There is, fortunately, no need to take sides. Both words translate to "water of life" and the corruption "whiskey" (or "whisky" according to which side of the Irish Sea you are) is a result. The appendage "punch" is even more misleading, being derived from the Hindustani "panch" meaning "five": a reference to the required number of ingredients for a respectable brew. In this regard it is usually associated with steaming bowls of hot toddy. The recipe that follows, however, is for a 58° proof all-purpose drink that demands to be rested for at least six weeks before use and which can be brought into play on any occasion.

Ingredients 4 oz. sugar, 2 fl. oz. green tea, 5 fl. oz. brandy, 17 fl. oz. whisky, the rind of two lemons, 6 cloves, 1 teaspoonful of all spice (alternatively known as Jamaica Pepper or Pimento).

Method   Assemble all the ingredients in a wide-mouthed, screw-capped, jar. Stir thoroughly and seal tightly. Allow to soak for at least six weeks, then strain off the liquor through several thicknesses of fine muslin and bottle.

VAN DER HUM   An old Netherlands herb liqueur, originally devised by that anonymous genius Mister What's-his-name as its title suggests, still made in Holland but more frequently associated with the Cloete family who have been producing it in South Africa for more than two-hundred years.

The Dutch recipe is based on Curacao liqueurs to which a fine, sharp mandarin flavour is added. The better-known South African version features the peel of "naartjes" or Cape oranges. The 57° proof recipe hereunder makes use of the more easily accessible peel of tangerines.

Ingredients   8 fl. oz. sugar-syrup, 26 fl. oz. brandy, 5 fl. oz. rum, 2 tablespoonfuls (1 oz.) of finely cut tangerine peel which must be free of all pith, one dessertspoonful (¼ oz.) of cinnamon, 5 cloves, a saltspoonful of powdered nutmeg, one or two cardamom seeds, and a dessertspoonful of dried orange flower petals.

Method   Slightly bruise the cloves and cardamom seeds before placing these, along with all the other dry ingredients, in a wide-mouthed screw-capped jar. Pour on the brandy, stir well and leave, tightly capped, for one month. It is important that the vessel should be completely air-tight and be given a daily shake to help things along. After one month, strain the liquor through several thicknesses of fine muslin and stir in the sugar-syrup. When this is completely incorporated, add the rum. Leave in a well-corked vessel for at least a further two weeks, again shaking daily. Finally, filter through coffee filter paper or a paper towel.

The ingredient proportions stated will provide approximately one-and-a-half standard bottles of liqueur.

Chapter IX

The Importance of Presentation

THERE are excellent home-made liqueurs and poor ones, often made from identical ingredients. The difference, more often than not, lies in the manner of their presentation.

These end pages, attributing a sense of social responsibility to their reader, aim to bridge that difference.

The art of dispensing anything so precious as a home-produced liqueur begins, logically enough, with the funnelling of the stuff into a bottle: not any old bottle but the most beautiful one you can find. Ideally it will be a bottle which, by deliberate intent through shape of form, catches the eye, holds the attention and demands closer acquaintance. For a source of supply, look to your local hotelier or restauranteur.

Such folk usually have a hotch-potch of suitable commercial empties cluttering up their premises and are generally glad to see the back of them.

Use no bottle because it happens to come conveniently to hand. Regard it from every angle, and if you don't consider it capable of standing comparison with any of the vessels ranged along the neon-lit shelving of the most exclusive hostelries, sling it! When, however, you come across something capable of being properly corked and so graceful that it whispers for a caress, earmark it for your very best. The material of which it may be made is not significant. Glass, of course, is the usual medium, varying from clear through frosted effects and the most delicate tints of green and golden-green to dark green and various shades of umber. Suitable containers of stone-ware, glazed pottery and even bone-china are not, however, unusual and, along with all types of heavily pigmented glassware, lend themselves admirably to the protection of their content's rich colour which may suffer if exposed to too much light.

Whatever sort of bottle is used it must be scrupulously clean; not only as regards its insides but to the extent of having its exterior surface so rinsed and polished that not so much as a gum smear remains to mark the passing of a previous label.

Generally speaking, sterilisation is unnecessary since liqueurs, containing well in excess of fourteen per cent alcohol by volume, are fully capable of looking after themselves. Working, however, to the yet-to-be-disproved maxim that it is better to be sure than sorry, the extra safety factor provided by a quick sulphite rinse may well be considered worthwhile. Four Campden tablets, crushed and dissolved in a pint of warm water, are merely swilled around the already cleaned bottle which should, then, be rinsed free of their pungent influence with a little boiled water that has been allowed to cool.

Immediately prior to the bottle being filled, a brief up-ending will permit any clinging drop of water to make its exit and the liqueur is then added to a level that allows about one inch of space below the point to which the bottom of the cork will reach.

Bottles designed to be sealed by means of a screw-on cap, though frequently employed for the marketing of spirits and many vermouths, are never satisfactory vessels for the proper promotion of a liqueur. Their general character is against them. They are just not right. Old corks, on the other hand, are probably sour and invariably loaded with all manner of contaminating influences. New ones should, therefore, always be used. These are available in a range of standard sizes and a choice of three shapes: straight-cylindrical, tapered or flanged. When selecting from these types bear in mind, however, that the cork most easily inserted is the one most likely to lose its grip. There is, thus, much to be said in favour of the straight-cylindrical pattern since this demands the use of a special tool (a corking-gun or hand-corker) if it is to be driven home flush to the neck of a bottle without a deal of messing.

Tapered corks do not require the assistance of any such gadget. They are merely inserted as far as possible and then thumped into place by means of a flogger (a short length of conveniently shaped one-inch board) or, more often, the heel of a lady's shoe. Alternatively, they can be urged fully home by being held against a wall whilst the bottle itself is pressed and twisted against any resistance they have to offer. In the event of air (trapped and compressed between the level of the bottle's contents and the base of the cork) acting as a buffer to spring the cork back as soon as the pressure against it is released, this difficulty may be overcome as follows:

Slip one end of a length of thin string down inside the neck of the vessel prior to the insertion of the cork. Then, when the latter is fully home, a steady pull on the free end withdraws the string and permits any built-up air pressure to escape.

Flanged stoppers (entirely made of cork or fitted with colourful plastic tops) are the easiest of all sealing devices to use and even obviate the necessity of having a screw to hand when opening time comes round. They are not, however, sufficiently reliable for the stoppaging of bottles left to mature in the horizontal and are inclined to seal themselves so securely under the influence of a liqueur's sugar content that they often break when an effort is made to remove them. All-plastic stoppers, which click home to a fair degree of security (and would not be so generally approved for commercial employment were it otherwise) are available for amateur use and have the advantage of being many times re-usable. One can, however, be so unfortunate as to come across an occasional leaker.

Where, then, does all this lead us? Ideally, to the application of a routine and choice of closures based on circumstance.

This may be charted as follows:

1. *Vessels intended for prolonged storage on their sides* – Use a straight-cylindrical cork, replacing this with an all-cork or plastic flanged stopper once it has been withdrawn and the bottle itself is on the sideboard and open to customers.

2. *Vessels containing liqueurs that are going to be dispensed within a matter of months* – Use a straight-cylindrical or tapered cork and keep a spare plastic closure handy in the sideboard's gadget drawer against the possibility of its breaking during extraction.

3. *Vessels intended for immediate service* – Flanged stoppers, cork or plastic, are perfectly satisfactory.

All corks should be softened before use. Left to soak for twenty-four hours in a little cold water to which a teaspoonful or so of glycerine has been added, they swell and become more manageable, adjusting themselves exactly to the dimensions of the neck into which they are forced. Plastic stoppers need only to be rinsed in a weak sulphite solution from time to time.

So much for the basic and inescapable preliminaries. Now for the final touches that, judiciously applied, make the bottle itself the focal-point of any occasion and the downing of its contents even downier. Coloured capsules are available for amateur use. One of these, slipped over a cork and bottle neck, adds an impressive touch of professional expertise and serves the practical purpose of providing a supplementary air seal in place of the wax coating once employed.

Capsules are of three main types, made of either metal-foil or plastic. The foil ones, internally coated with a thin adhesive, are casually but centrally cupped over the cork and bottle neck which need to have been previously moistened by means of a squeezed-out scrap of cotton-wool. The rolling action of a tight rubber ring then crimps the pre-formed pleating of the capsule accurately into place. The plastic sort, though similar as regards intent, divide into two distinct groups identified by the names "Viscose" and "Visplas" respectively.

Viscose capsules are fairly fragile, being easily torn during application, and need to be kept softened in a special solution or they dry to shrivelled shapes that defy reconstitution. Maintained under the right conditions, however, they are thin pockets of a flexible material capable of incredible shrinkage. Thus within an hour or so of their being placed over the business end of any vessel, cork and neck are completely encased in a tight protective skin exactly contoured to their shape. Visplas capsules, on the other hand, are rugged and retain their moulded form under all circumstances. A quick plunge into hot water provides a temporary softening that enables them to be urged and twisted over the neck of a bottle which, from that point on, they grip beyond the point of casual removal. All types have their followers and critics but whichever sort is used it is worthwhile to rub the top edge of any newly opened bottle with a piece of waxed paper prior to dispensing its contents. This prevents dripping. To further avoid spillage, twist the bottle to left or right as you complete the pouring operation.

The application of a good label depends for its effect on neatness and legibility rather than any particular artistic skill on the part of its designer. Size and shape are important. These should be appropriate to the dimensions of the bottle; neither so small that the label appears dominated, nor so large that the label obscures the major bulk of the liqueur it identifies.

Pot-bellied containers and vessels principally made up of curved surfaces (which look delightful) invariably occasion presentation problems since no label can be expected to lie flat against them. These, therefore, look their best when dressed with a narrow (three-quarter inch) overlapping scarf of paper around their shoulders. The details of their content can then be printed centrally on the overlap. In all other cases labels need to be so placed that their top edge never extends higher than about one-and-a-half inches below the shoulder; widthwise they should be capable of a central position between the seams of the bottle so that they are wholly visible by a single frontal glance. If a bottle needs to be turned so that its label may be read, we're back in the sauce-bottle class and the whole purpose of our presentation is defeated.

A considerable range of colourful and well-designed bottle-label blanks, of all shapes and sizes, is available for amateur use. These merely require to be completed with such details as may be considered appropriate. In this regard, however, the majority of folk (lacking any skill in penmanship, virtually inseparable from a ball-point and perhaps disinclined to involve the expense of a special over-printing) are in some difficulty. The result, more often than not, is a handsome setting marred by a straggle of ill-formed and indecipherable handwriting: a touch of individuality which the majority of us are prepared to forgo.

A simple remedy lies in the use of dry-transfer lettering sheets, sold for student use by most good stationers and art shops, and providing the means of producing an effect indistinguishable from the finest letter-press or offset. Detailed instructions are, of course, provided but the whole process, from first to last, involves no more than the removal of a siliconized backing paper, the positioning of any letter required by means of an in-built spacing guide, and the application of a light pressure to the back of the sheet. So, letter by letter, the required wording is built up.

The time taken for the production of a complete label must inevitably depend upon the amount of information it needs to carry. In no case should more than half-an-hour or so be involved.

Then, faced with a thin protective plastic and adhered by means of a peelable photo-mountant, it will serve many times over to be passed from bottle to bottle, eventually coming to rest, perhaps, between the pages of a winery record: a happy reminder of past loves and the inspiration of future triumphs.

APPENDIX

Formulation for the assessment of the alcohol strength of a wine sweetened either by the addition of a standard sugar-syrup or any quantity of sugar in its solid form, dissolved into the liquor under the influence of gentle heat and continuous stirring:

$$\frac{A \times B}{C} \quad \text{where} \quad \begin{array}{l} A = \text{No. of oz. of wine prior to sweetening addition} \\ B = \text{Alcohol strength of wine} \\ C = \text{No. of oz. sweetened wine} \end{array}$$

Example 1. 10 fl. oz. of wine having a strength of 21° proof are sweetened by the addition of 3 fl. oz. of sugar-syrup.

Then $\dfrac{10 \times 21}{10 + 3} = \dfrac{210}{13} = 16.15°$ proof or, near enough, 16° proof

Example 2. 10 oz. of granulated sugar are dissolved into 15 fl. oz. of a 21° proof wine the volume of which is thus increased by 6¼ fl. oz. to a total of 21¼ fl. oz.

$$\frac{15 \times 21}{21.25} = \frac{315}{21.25} = 14.82° \text{ proof or, near enough, } 15° \text{ proof}$$

Formula for the assessment of the final strength of a liqueur blended from a sweetened wine and any strength of fortifying spirit:

$$\frac{(C \times D) + (E \times F)}{G} \quad \text{where} \quad \begin{array}{l} C = \text{No. of oz. sweetened wine} \\ D = \text{Alcohol strength of sweetened wine} \\ E = \text{No. of oz. fortifying spirit} \\ F = \text{Alcohol strength of fortifying spirit} \\ G = \text{Total volume of sweetened wine and fortifying spirit in combination} \end{array}$$

156

Example 13 fl. oz. of a sweetened wine (assessed to have a strength of 16° proof in accordance with the workings of Example 1 above) are combined with 13 fl. oz. of a 68° proof vodka.

Then:

$$\frac{(13 \times 16) + (13 \times 68)}{26} = \frac{208 + 884}{26} = \frac{1092}{26} = 42° \text{ proof}$$

INDEX

160

Other titles in the Amateur Winemaker Series

AMATEUR WINEMAKER RECIPES (Edited by C.J.J. BERRY)
Recipes from the monthly magazine, 'Amateur Winemaker'. Over
200 are gathered together here in one vital reference.

BETTER COUNTRY WINES (P.W. TOMBS)
A comprehensive, down-to-earth book which not only describes
successful wines but advises what to avoid and how to prevent or
cure disorders in winemaking. Includes over 100 recipes plus
suggestions for experiment and variation.

BETTER WINES FROM CONCENTRATES (T. EDWIN BELT)
This remarkable book includes day-by-day detailed instructions on
processing and over 300 recipes for all types of wine, punches, cups
and coolers, cordials, cocktails, vermouths, liqueurs etc., with
additional information on serving, wine and cheese, even tobacco
fermenting.

GREAT FERMENTATIONS (MARION WHITTOW)
Marion Whittow relates her winemaking experience on this useful
and amusing book. Her advice on the home winemaking process is
full of commonsense and her witty cartoons enliven the text.

HOW TO MAKE WINES WITH A SPARKLE
(JOHN RESTALL and DON HOBBS)
Discover the secrets of producing champagne-like wine of superb
quality. The natural choice for celebrations and festive occasions,
sparkling wines have a place in everybody's winery, and now the
amateur winemaker who follows this book's methods can produce
them for himself.

100 WINEMAKING PROBLEMS ANSWERED (CEDRIC AUSTIN)
Cedric Austin answers a selection of questions put to him over the
years on the most frequent problems encountered by amateur
winemakers.

130 NEW WINEMAKING RECIPES (C.J.J. BERRY)
Contains tests and reliable recipes, many of which are unique to this
publication, but certain well-tried favourites are also included.

MAKING WINES LIKE THOSE YOU BUY
(BRYAN ACTON and PETER DUNCAN)
How to reproduce the flavour and quality of commercial wines in your own home. Sauternes, hocks, Madeiras and champagne are all possibilities with the help of this book.

MODERN WINEMAKING TECHNIQUES (GLADYS BLACKLOCK)
Explains clearly and concisely how to obtain the best results from a wide range of ingredients.

PROGRESSIVE WINEMAKING
(PETER DUNCAN and BRYAN ACTON)
This book is the outcome of many years practical experience of winemaking at home, and its whole emphasis is upon producing quality wines which will bear full comparison with the popular wines of the Continent. It shows clearly the path to advanced winemaking, and consequently will be warmly welcomed by those who already know something of the subject, but it will also prove invaluable to the complete beginner, for whom typical recipes have been included. Every aspect of winemaking is covered thoroughly.

RECIPES FOR PRIZEWINNING WINES (BRYAN ACTON)
Nearly all these recipes have won prizes at national and regional shows and the amateur who follows them carefully will produce high quality wines with the minimum of effort and the maximum of certainty.

SCIENTIFIC WINEMAKING – MADE EASY
(J.R. MITCHELL and T. TIMBRELL)
The author was a quality control executive at one of the largest British beverage firms, and thus ideally qualified to write such a book. 2nd edition in preparation, due March 1987.

THE WINEMAKER'S DICTIONARY (PETER McCALL)
A comprehensive A-Z of the art and science of winemaking from the preparation of the ingredients to decanting the resultant wine. Thorough cross-referencing and a systematic approach make this an indispensible reference book for all winemakers.

WINEMAKER'S COMPANION (C.J.J. BERRY and BEN TURNER)
This book gives a sensible and practical explanation of what modern winemaking is all about, and describes the basic principles, main ingredients, equipment required, and processes for making wines and beers of good quality. It deals in detail with the making of an individual wine and gives recipes for many more, using fruit and certain other ingredients which the authors have found to be successful. Subjects also dealt with are cellarcraft, the serving and appreciation of wine, keeping records and how to take part in competitions. As well as covering every aspect of the hobby, this also makes an excellent reference book.

WINEMAKING SIMPLIFIED (E.H. CORNISH)
Designed to encourage the beginner rather than blind him with science, this book uses one man's practical experience to give guidance to successful winemaking.

WINEMAKING WITH CANNED & DRIED FRUIT (C.J.J. BERRY)
Easy, clean and economical, this simple system of winemaking will appeal to everyone. This book tells how to make delightful wines from low-price ingredients from markets, grocers and chemists.

WINEMAKING WITH CONCENTRATES (PETER DUNCAN)
Invaluable to the flat dweller who enjoys wine but lacks the facilities to make it from grapes and other fruits, and to any winemaker who uses concentrates.

WINEMAKING WITH ELDERBERRIES (T. EDWIN BELT)
Elderberry wine is a great favourite, with the fruit available for anyone to gather from the countryside. Describes the different varieties of fruit and ways to make the best of them.

WORLDWIDE WINEMAKING RECIPES (ROY EKINS)
This intriguing book gives dozens of original recipes for unusual wines – Ugli, Dingleberry and many more.

ALL ABOUT BEER & HOME BREWING (BOB PRITCHARD)
Bob Pritchard has spent his working life in the brewing trade and was in at the start of the homebrewing boom when it took off in the 60s. His vast knowledge and experience are condensed into this book.

BEER KITS AND BREWING (DAVE LINE)
All the latest information on beer kits, hopped worts, malt extract and the new equipment is here, set out clearly in a manner which will appeal to the beginner and enthusiast alike.

THE BIG BOOK OF BREWING (DAVE LINE)
This definitive handbook covers every aspect of homebrewing. Traditional techniques used to brew the finest beers and ales are adapted for the amateur and described with authority and humour.

BREWER'S DICTIONARY (PETER D. McCALL)
This book has around 1300 entries covering all apects of brewing and giving explanations on technical terms and different beer types. Ingredients for brewing are dealt with in detail, for example there are 79 entries covering the necessary information on hops. Everything is clearly presented in alphabetical order and extensive cross referencing leads the reader to related topics.

BREWING BEERS LIKE THOSE YOU BUY (DAVE LINE)
There's a good chance you'll find your favourite brew here – now you can learn how to brew it at home at a fraction of the pub cost! Recipes have been extracted from information given by the breweries themselves about their beers.

BREWING BETTER BEERS (KEN SHALES)
The complete guide for the advanced enthusiast. All the recipes have been repeatedly tested and can be relied on to produce beers of superb quality, true to type.

BREWING LAGER (J. ALEXANDER)
This is the only book which deals solely with larger brewing and covers every stage in detail. There is an explanation of the various types of lager and the necessary ingredients, with details on refridgeration, bottling and casking methods. The beginner is taken step by step through the first brew onto making genuine continental lager. A number of recipes, suitable for the beginner and the experienced brewer, are also included.

THE HAPPY BREWER (WILF NEWSOM)
The home brewer who wishes to go more deeply into the theory and techniques of brewing will find all the answers in this book.

HINTS ON HOME BREWING (C.J.J. BERRY)
Provides step-by-step instruction on various methods and guides the amateur in selection of equipment and ingredients. 150,000 copies sold.

HOME BREWED BEERS AND STOUTS (C.J.J. BERRY)
The first modern book on home brewing, this was an instant success when it was first published in 1963. This latest edition contains up-to-date information on how to brew fine beers and stouts of authentic flavour and strength for as little as 6p a pint! Send S.A.E. for our current price list.

HOME BREWING FOR AMERICANS (DAVID MILLER)
Here are simple ways to brew all kinds of beers from American malts. Fifteen fully detailed recipes through Light to Dark Lagers, Ales and Bitters, Porter and Stout.

BE A WINE AND BEER JUDGE (S.W. ANDREWS)
The author was the founder chairman of the Amateur Winemakers National Guild of Judges. In his book he advises the proficient amateur on the right steps to take to qualify as an officially recognised wine judge.

SUGAR-FREE WINES AND BEERS (PETER D. McCALL)
With an increasing concern about diet and heatlh, this book has been written to enable winemakers and brewers to produce sugar-free wines and beers. It covers aspects of health related to wine and beer making and has an extensive section on diabetes.

GROWING VINES (NICK POULTER)
Down to earth advice, a guide to vine varieties and a 'through the year' diary are all there to help the enthusiast succeeded in this exciting new venture.

MAKING CIDER (JO DEAL)
Describes how, with the minimum of equipment, a glut of apples can be converted into delicious cider for drinking and culinary use.

MAKING INEXPENSIVE LIQUEURS (REN BELLIS)
The gamut of exotic liqueurs is described, then the reader is initiated into how to reproduce these flavours and textures for himself.

MAKING MEAD (BRYAN ACTON and PETER DUNCAN)
This is an informative and entertaining guide to one of the world's oldest crafts. It combines ancient and modern techniques to give today's reader the complete mead-making picture.

VINES IN YOUR GARDEN (JAMES PAGE-ROBERTS)
This is the book for those with a little garden space who wish to make their own wine and eat their own grapes. The author's clear, step-by-step approach is complemented by his explanatory diagrams and illustrations by Bernard Venables.

WINES FROM YOUR VINES (NICK POULTER)
The sequel to 'Growing Vines', this book goes on to help the viticulturist make the most of his harvest by setting out in a detailed and practical way instructions on all aspects of winemaking from grapes.

WOODWORK FOR WINEMAKERS (C.J. DART and D.A. SMITH)
The authors combine their knowledge of woodworking and wine-making to show the amateur winemaker how to build his own equipment. Be it a winepress, fruit pulper or winery, the instructions are all here, with clear, detailed working drawings to help you succeed.

FIRST STEPS IN WINEMAKING (C.J.J.BERRY)
Universally known as 'the Winemaker's Bible', this book is an inspiration to beginners in winemaking. It covers terminology, basic facts and techniques and also gives an invaluable month by month guide to seasonal recipes for wine. There is also advice on the social side of the hobby – wine circles and competitions.